Parenting

Discover How to Teach Your Angry Child to Deal

(A Modern Guide to Understand and Raise Your Asd Child to Success)

Bonnie Pospisil

Published By **Chris David**

Bonnie Pospisil

Parenting: Discover How to Teach Your Angry Child to Deal (A Modern Guide to Understand and Raise Your Asd Child to Success)

ISBN 978-1-998769-35-3

Legal & Disclaimer

The information contained in this ebook is not designed to replace or take the place of any form of medicine or professional medical advice. The information in this ebook has been provided for educational & entertainment purposes only.

The information contained in this book has been compiled from sources deemed reliable, and it is accurate to the best of the Author's knowledge; however, the Author cannot guarantee its accuracy and validity and cannot be held liable for any errors or omissions. Changes are periodically made to this book. You must consult your doctor or get professional medical advice before using any of the suggested remedies, techniques, or information in this book.

Upon using the information contained in this book, you agree to hold harmless the Author from and against any damages, costs, and expenses, including any legal fees potentially resulting from the application of any of the information provided by this guide. This disclaimer applies to any damages or injury caused by the use and application, whether directly or indirectly, of any advice or information presented, whether for breach of contract, tort, negligence, personal injury, criminal intent, or under any other cause of action.

You agree to accept all risks of using the information presented inside this book. You need to consult a professional medical practitioner in order to ensure you are both able and healthy enough to participate in this program.

Table of contents

Chapter 1: What Is Reactive Parenting?

Reactive parenting means parenting that is driven by extreme emotion in response to a child's misbehavior. This parenting approach often results in severe punishment and anger from both the parent or the child.

You can yell, scream, or hit your child impulsively if you are frustrated with their behavior. Reactive parenting is not a good idea. They will be constantly frustrated at their child's behavior. Reactive parenting means that parents look out for their child's misbehavior and not enjoy their time with their children.

Reactive parenting leads to emotional harm for their children as well as harming the parent-child relationship. It teaches children how manipulate their behavior. It is like your child believes you're manipulating them. If this continues, your child may have difficulty learning right from wrong. They will want to please you so don't react too much.

Your child throwing a temper tantrum or throwing up on the floor could leave you confused as to what to do. It is likely that no matter what you do, temper tantrums will cause your child to lose control.

It is difficult to ignore your feelings when your children are crying or acting in a way that is not right for you. Frustration can build up over time, which can lead to irritation and aggravation. Sometimes it is easy to become emotional, allowing your emotions and reactions to your child's misbehavior to guide your actions.

You don't need to be a reactive parent. Being a calmer parent can help you be more peaceful every day.

Teaching your child the difference between right and wrong requires thinking abilities. Children will learn to be more than just impressed by you if they are motivated by good behavior. Reacting to everything will make it difficult for your child to see the limit of what they can accomplish before you get tired of them.

What happens if you're not there? So what's their motivation?

What Factors Influence Reactive Parenting

Research has shown that three factors can impact the parenting style and behavior of parents. They are: The character of the child and the personality of parents.

Some parents react to their children's behavior and adopt a reactive parenting style. They tend to view the child’s misbehaviors as malicious. This can have a significant impact on the parents' responses.

Parents who feel that their child is acting out of malice will be more harsh with their children. An unreactive parent will believe that the child's tantrum may be more than what they are doing.

Parents who feel their child is not being responsible and are incapable of self-control will react negatively to this behavior.

Parenting is a holy calling. There are two options: you can be a reactive or non-reactive parent. Be aware that your actions have an effect on the children.

Chapter 2: Reactive Parenting Triggers

A trigger is any experience that causes you to feel repressed feelings from the past. This is when we react in ways that contradict the present.

A trigger can be used to open up a childhood hurt, such as feeling unheard or not valued. We constantly seek out confirmation that this world is what it is. This wound is a story we tell to ourselves that we believe is true. This famous story is a reminder of how we feel when we are not heard, like when we ask our child to join me for dinner. What if you feel unheard as a child? You are angry and unsatisfied.

These old, forgotten emotions can bring out negative emotions that can lead to irritability and anger. You can't bond with your child if they are considered enemies.

Perhaps your child reminds you of a parent or sibling that you are struggling with. The most common trigger for this is when the child makes one think about themselves, someone, or something they dislike.

You don't have need to look into your past in order to become a great parent. It is important to be able recognize your triggers. It is possible to find tiny, upsetting things or sensitive topics that trigger your trauma. Parents might find their child’s conduct troubling even if it doesn’t address the major problems.

Nobody enjoys being ignored. No one likes to be ignored. Certain behavior are universally accepted and would drive anyone crazy.

6 Triggers to Reactive Parenting

Are you losing your anger more often than usual? Here are six parenting stressors that are most prevalent and tips to deal with them.

1. Whining

You need to be able to control your emotions and not let your child whine. It can be a frustrating trigger for you because it frustrates your child. Wailing children are upsetting, especially when you have a lot to do.

Before reacting, be honest with yourself and acknowledge that you are being triggered.

Remember that your brain is only software. Your brain has been functioning in this way all your life. However, it doesn't need to continue functioning in this manner. It is possible to change your behavior. Although ranting and losing your cool is not something you are naturally inclined to do, it can help strengthen your brain.

2. Disrespectfulness

Many of us have experienced disrespect in our childhoods, which can lead to us becoming angry when our children treat others disrespectfully. Insolence and anger can lead to a parent becoming entangled in an ineffective power struggle. If you weren't feeling triggered, your brain would switch to problem-solving mode. It may be that you will never want brushing your teeth again, as you have grown to hate it. Failure to brush your teeth can lead your teeth becoming infected, and then eventually falling out.

Your child can choose to brush their own teeth in the bathroom, or in the kitchen. This is much better than holding your child's hand while you brush their tooth, as our parents did. Engaging in a power struggle makes a child feel weaker. In the future, they are more likely to use disdainfulness to gain control of you.

3. "I Hate You!"

Most parents feel triggered when their children tell them, "I hate your!" This is a sign that the child is trying the worst, most explosive thing to get their anger at you.

Hatred can be a perception of something, not a fact. If a child shouts, "I hate!" They are not saying they hate you, but their parents. They are actually saying: I'm so miserable; I'm afraid we'll never work things out together.

What is an appropriate response? You can be angry with me as much as you wish. You'll always be loved by me. "But you cannot have another cookie.

4. Suffering a physical injury

Parents get angry when their children cause harm to them. Children might take a lot of measures to catch our attention. Your child may headbutt you while trying to get into their car seat.

It's perfectly normal to get angry from time-to-time. If you have time to let your temper cool down, it's crucial to mend the relationship. Natural clashes and healthy fights such as your spouse shouting at you because they are being mistreated, are part in life. Your actions can have serious consequences. These stimuli trigger normal human emotions. They do not have anything to do with being bad, tired, harsh or having been through trauma. They are simply awful things that make you feel terrible.

5. Rivalry between siblings

Sibling rivalry can also be a trigger. Parents react if one of their children is hurtful or hostile. Perhaps it is related to how your family used to function when you were a kid, or if one of your siblings did things that you did not.

Naturally, you will react defensively. Both protection and compassion both have their place. We need to believe our children are more powerful than we think and we shouldn't be ashamed of growing furious at them.

If one sibling is constantly annoying another, it is essential to establish boundaries. It is your duty to protect one sibling and establish boundaries with the others.

6. Spills and Mistakes

While everyone responds differently to triggers, they all have different triggers. An orderly and organized person would not feel triggered by a child making mistakes.

When your child makes a mistake or spills something on you, it is likely that you are feeling triggered. Most likely it was an emergency.

Is this really a crisis or not?

No.

If you're accustomed to reacting to mistakes or spills with anger, try a different approach. Take a moment to let the pressure off your chest, relax your shoulders, and allow your mouth to open. It could be, "It's OK people, spills happen. This happens to everyone, we'll clean it all up.

It will become second nature after some practice. You can talk to your child later about spill avoidance techniques.

Chapter 3: Effects Of Reactive Parenting On Children Into Adulthood

Research suggests that children who exhibit anger and aggression are more likely to be irritated by their parents.

This research is necessary to understand the complex connection between genetics and childhood. Researchers from Oregon State University, Oregon Social Learning Center, as well as other institutions, gathered data on 361 families that had adopted from ten different states. They also obtained genetic details from the biological parents.

They assessed the children at 9 and 18 months. The study found that children with adoptive parents who reacted quickly and became upset when their children broke the rules or made mistakes were more likely to exhibit 'negative emotions' and more tantrums than expected.

Genetics also played a part, especially for children who inherited the tendency to have negative emotions from their mother but were raised with low stress or less reactive environments.

Research shows that children who experience more negative emotions in the early years of their lives are more likely than others to struggle to cope with these emotions later on and are more likely engage in dangerous behavior.

Researchers also discovered that children who experienced the greatest increase in negative emotions as they aged from infants and toddlers (between 9 and 27 months), also had the highest levels problem behaviors at the tender age of 2. This suggests that negative feelings may be part of a separate developmental process which influences their later behavior.

This aspect of emotion was thought to be relatively stable by researchers. This research still shows that even though most children experience more negative emotions as they grow up, their behavior as toddlers can be affected by how they test boundaries.

Parents of babies and young children can learn a lot from their toddlers. How they adjust to toddlerhood, which is often a challenging time marked by independence and growing mobility, may have an impact on their child's development.

Parents can help their children change their behavior. A way to help your children do this is to learn how you manage yourself. Be steady, confident and don't react too much. You are the parent. Your actions and emotions will set the example.

Most parents are aware that self-control plays a vital role in a happy and healthy childhood. Children who lack this support are more likely to lose their emotional stability from peer provocation and criticism. But, parents often neglect to promote parental self-control. It is vital in building this social and emotional foundation. Instead of setting a positive example, reactive parents can lose their cool when dealing with hyperactive kids. Reactive parenting does not teach self-control.

Reactive parenting often results from childhood experiences. As parents raise children, tolerance is checked on a daily basis. This could "open windows into" one's teenage years.

Parents who use intimidation or terror to raise their children will practice reactive parenting. Instead of prioritizing safety or self-correction and two way communication between parent and child (or both), the parent resorts instead to yelling at and punishing. People who understand the harm this punishing parenting style can have on children are more willing to explore other options.

Preparing for rapid cooling means focusing on your child's behavior and identifying your parenting hotspots. Disobedience is a trigger. These behaviors are part of parenting and not an indication that you're becoming an unlogical parent.

Be a parent coach, not a cop. A parent cop tends to emphasize threats and punishments as the primary instructional strategy. A parent coach sees children's mistakes as opportunities to learn self-correction. This strategy requires that you listen to your children, be open to their opinions, provide solutions and demonstrate understanding. You should remember that understanding is not the equivalent of agreeing. In describing punishments, be sure to emphasize the detrimental impact that bad behavior can have on privileges, trust and unexpected surprises.

You can use a soothing voice and words that promote two-way communication. One way to get a good coaching meeting started is with the phrase "Let's figure out how can we handle this problem without losing control" This level of openness decreases the child's defensiveness. It prevents reactive parenting mistakes like accusing, manipulating, blaming and manipulating (the other A.B.C.s).

Keep in mind that any unacceptable behavior serves to communicate a message. The parent has the responsibility to interpret that message so that communication can be more effective. Stress the importance of communicating effectively with your child using the right tone, words, & actions. You can discuss these issues with your child, even when you're not there. This will let them know that you are interested in their growth and is a way to show that they care.

Stop using reactive parenting techniques in your family and you will see a change in how everyone feels.

Chapter 4: How To Stop Letting Your Children Down

It's not good to lose your temper and shout at children. This doesn't necessarily make you a bad parent.

You will not automatically stop falling in love with your child. It would be unreasonable to expect such a thing. You would snap less often and, with these skills and strategies, you can recuperate more quickly and thoroughly.

How can I control my anger and keep it from getting out of control?

It is possible to hold ourselves responsible by understanding our triggers, and setting up internal 'failsafes. Parents are often unable to control their stress levels when it activates the brain's automatic flight, fight or freeze response.

We don't choose to be a loser with our kids. It is very difficult to say no to something you don't want.

Eight ways you can stop losing your mind with your child

Parents cannot decide not to lose the sh*t. However if parents pay attention and notice triggers, it is possible to prevent your child losing their shit with you or reduce its impact.

What can I do?

Many!

Here are eight strategies for managing your anger and keeping calm around children.

1. Recognize that willpower cannot be used effectively.

Stress triggers the fight/flight response. It also inhibits the prefrontal cortex, which is the part that controls our ability to evaluate and plan for our emotions.

It's impossible to argue with yourself when you are having a lose-yourself moment. Even if it were possible, the neurological system in a human being is not able to respond to orders. Your nervous system will recognize your increased tension as a sign you are in danger and attempt to manage it.

2. Take note of your triggers, and remember to practice pausing.

It can be helpful to identify the moments just before your parents meltdowns. You have to recognize that you are about lose your shit. It is important to pay attention how you act within the time you have left before you lose it.

The next important step is to break. If there was a threat to our safety, we wouldn't allow ourselves to take a short break. This is a vital message to our nervous system stating that this is not a threat.

Continue to inhale and outhale gently throughout the pause. Deep breathing can be compared to hacking your brain. Deep breathing allows you to urge your nervous systems not to panic. You'll be fine, I promise.

3. Find a Vent.

Pausing may help you get out a reaction. But your engines keep going at full speed, as though you're racing into space. Power and momentum don't disappear on their own. They must be released. The next step after stopping and breathing is to do something else.

You still have incredible energy and are ready to fight, or run. You have to do something to harness that energy. Triggering is a body's bodily reaction to the situation. This could be physical activity, saying prayers, singing a tune, or simply repeating a mantra.

4. Multitasking should not be attempted.

If you want to be a good parent, it is important to focus on one thing at once. These words may be contradictory for working parents who are used to spending months at a time, with one eye on a phone and the other on their child. With so many tasks competing for our attention, we are less likely and more likely not to accomplish what we need to do.

Multitasking is not something humans can do. Our brains are not made to be multitasking. This is why we sometimes think we can do two tasks at once. Our brain jumps between activities, so some parts of the brain or even our body may not catch up. This leads to a perception of too many balls in the air, and we may lose one. It triggers our emotions and increases the chance that we snap at our children.

5. Take time to spend quality time with your kids.

Multitasking is rarely productive. Multitasking is impossible when you have to pay attention to your children and work at multiple jobs.

Imagine your children playing while you clean the dishes and answer email. This will make you anxious and make you more susceptible to throwing tantrums. It's better to be present or absent than to fluctuate with your children. Give your children 20-30 mins of your total attention. Tell your children that you need to be working, and now is the best time for screen time. You could also read a book, or have us prepare an activity or craft. Now, it's time to take on some tasks.

6. Teach Your Children To Be Patient

Many parents feel embarrassed to tell their children they need to take time for grownups. It makes them feel bad and like they're not doing enough. She believes that telling children not to rush is better for both parents as well as children.

Your child's safety is at stake if you are not available. Children may not be able to solve problems by themselves if their parents aren't there. You can simply say, "OK, friend. It takes me five minutes to complete the email before I can assist you."

It takes time for children to learn that you aren't always available to satisfy their demands. However, you can start to educate your children about this early on. For some children it is easier because they prefer to play with their siblings or by themselves.

Certain children will find it more difficult. It can be more difficult for certain children to let you go if they are triggered - tired, anxious, terrified, or unhappy.

When you see your child excel at an autonomous task, don't be discouraged. Do not interrupt their child's fun. Allow them to be.

7. Do not use your phone.

Parents are often furious with their kids and reach for their phones frequently when it is. Although phones may allow us to escape from the present moment, they are more likely than not to worsen it.

Simply put your smartphone down.

Our phones can be very triggery. Stop scrolling to the point of disaster. You are more likely to be entertained and informed by what you see on your phone than what is going on in your life. When your child asks for your attention and sees a funny movie, you might ignore him or her.

8. Don't rush to find a solution.

Parents often try to resolve conflicts too quickly once they become heated. It's not likely that you can reconcile with your child if they remain unhappy. You're assuming your child will accept your apology. This will not happen because they are kids. They worry too much and don't need to.

Your child is either sad or has moved on. You may find that they are constantly irritating you because they do the same things you did. You might feel angry at them or try to get them to understand.

Chapter 5: Non-Reactive Parenting

Non-reactive parenthood doesn't have to be emotionless. Non-reactive means responsive and intentional parenting.

Use non-reactive parenthood as a parenting strategy. It is crucial to not act out adult emotions such anger. It is difficult to master and contradictory.

It is possible to calm a hyperactive child with non-reactive parenting.

Non-reactive parenting can be described as the antithesis of reactive parenting.

Reactive parenting refers to when emotions affect adult behavior and responses. Reactive parenting involves reacting violently to parenting difficulties by punishing or yelling out in anger.

It is acceptable to be angry or upset. Non-reactive parenthood means being calm. You can feel emotions and not react to them.

I've used non-reactive parenting techniques such as stopping, estimating alerting and acting (Taking an S.E.A.T.). I've used it so many times that it has become a daily routine.

Non-reaction does NOT mean there is no punishment. It is a punitive measure that is not motivated primarily by rage. It does not apply to children who are screaming, begging, or asking questions.

It is about adults managing their emotions and not children "getting away with it." An unhappy parent will need non-reactive parenting strategies. Rageful adults, however, will not help.

At one point, reactive parenting was a common practice. After reading this book you could shout at the child. You don't have to be afraid to "fail," as a parent. Do not be afraid to fail again.

Predisposed to seek caregiver connection for infants and toddlers, both positive and negative (anything except disengagement).

The fundamental study of this phenomenon found that babies were driven from neutral to pleasurable facial expressions.

Children are encouraged by their parents to encourage them to do the same things that get the best response.

Reactive parenting creates power struggles that older siblings can see. It is impossible to have a power battle if one side doesn't participate. If only one person is involved, there is nothing to be gained. Non-reactive parenting allows the adult to disrupt the power struggles that are all too common.

Yelling at children older than you causes them to behave the same (yelling in their face).

If you keep your cool with your child, communication with them as teenagers will be easier.

These strategies should permeate all aspects of your life. Negative emotions are for losers.

Non-Reactive Parenting Strategies

H.A.L.T (Hungry, Angry, Lonely, Tired)

When they're tired, hungry, lonely, or angry, no one can be at their best. Children and adults have more trouble controlling their behaviour and paying attention.

It is harder to parent when you are not able to respond in these situations.

It is vital to plan activities like meals and snacks for children and adults.

Credit is important

Reacting positively to unacceptable behavior is part of non reactive parenting.

To ensure non-reactive parenting, credit should be given to your child. This does not refer to a casual "good job," but rather intentional praise.

Be open to trying again

Non-reactive parenting works best with young children. This is because they're all brand new and gleaming and are free from any established patterns or habits and power plays.

It may take longer time to find the benefits from non-reactive parenting strategies with older children. It may take longer to discover the benefits of non-reactive parenting with older children.

Some families had a difficult time waiting for visible improvements. Do not stop trying. It is important that the parent's efforts are prioritized over the child's performance.

For anger management, calm your children by using non-reactive parentage

Sometimes, it's difficult to be a nonreactive father. You can still learn it.

It's not enough to be silent. You must consider your reactions and avoid reacting immediately to any adult behavior.

19 Ways You Can Become a Non Reactive Parent

Here are 20 tips for parents and daily life to avoid being too reactive.

1. You don't have to assume the worst.

Your children are your most important asset. Do you have a good relationship with your children? They offer everything they can.

2. Keep your eye on the goal.

Do you want to raise children who are quick to judge others and get furious at slight inconveniences?

Or?

Do you want your children to be happy and well-behaved?

3. A proactive mindset is essential.

Be proactive and make changes, not react to problems after they have occurred.

Instead of constantly feeling out-of-control, you should be in control of the situation.

4. Give your child the freedom and space to become an independent adult.

Children don't grow up to be more responsible and independent overnight. They will make mistakes as much as you at one point in your lives.

5. Be compassionate for your child.

Are they trying to imply something other than what they really meant? Are they tired, or do they have little time? Do they value your love and support more than your criticisms or punishments?

6. Think about a variety reaction.

What would the most caring parent in the world react to the same situation as you? What are your options now? Keep in mind that you do have choices.

7. Develop self-control

It's possible! Reactive parenting is associated with a lack or control and the tendency to respond without properly assessing the issue.

Take some time to pause, and then halt.

What will be the impact of your negative response to the issue?

8. Your current mental state is important.

Are you under pressure? Is it true? If so, how can you reduce it? Do you feel exhausted or irritable? Is it possible to reduce your exhaustion in this scenario? Do you have a soft spot? You might be a soft-spoken person.

9. Recognize that overreacting will make you feel powerless.

When you don't think before responding, you are reducing your power. You control your moods, emotions, and thoughts.

However, proactiveness helps you feel and control the issue.

10. Take stock of your expectations.

Are they trustworthy? Are they credible? Do you expect perfect behavior?

Expecting your child to do whatever you like is a recipe of disaster.

11. Be kind to your kids

Children are still growing. If you model kindness, love, forgiveness and kindness for your children, it can help them learn compassion, love, forgiveness, kindness, and compassion.

12. Recognize and accept the consequences of reactive parenthood.

Research suggests that children who exhibit anger and are quick to get upset have parents who are easily frustrated and react quickly.

13. Recognize it's not all about you!

Your responsibility as a parent is for your child to succeed in life.

Do your actions show that you support your children's efforts? Do you show kindness and love to others?

If not, it is time to review your default parenting solutions.

14. It is impossible to control the thoughts and feelings of your children.

Your children cannot be disciplined to follow your wishes. Research shows that unjust punishments only foster resentment. Every parenting situation can be handled better and more fairly.

15. Respect your child's personality and their character.

Your lively and outgoing toddler cannot suddenly be quiet. You can't expect a toddler who is active and excited to be sedentary all the time.

This is related back to the previous point concerning setting reasonable expectations.

Are your expectations realistic and in line with the abilities of your children?

16. If your child is acting out, the problem isn't with them.

Look at the action, not the individual. The child should be punished for their actions, not the one they are doing. Don't give your child a label they can't remove.

Don't give your child poor reputation to carry around with them wherever they go. Be aware that angry children are the result of angry parents. If you find yourself being too reactive makes you angry, then this article is for your. An angry mother is often the cause of anger in an angry child. It is better to control your anger than to allow it control you.

17. Relax.

STOP when you feel the need for a response.

How can I control the flame so it doesn't spread like wildfire?

You can reply in the non-reactive way in the same manner.

18. Don't let one bad day convince you that your parenting and life are not good.

The beauty of life lies in the fact that you can change your outlook at any moment, and your conduct as well.

19. Keep your cool first.

You can keep calm, think calmly, act calmly and love with gentleness.

You have the power to decide how you react to your child's behavior. If you have the option, choose tranquility.

Chapter 6: How To Effectively Communicate With Your Children

Every day is a new opportunity to communicate with your child. Parents are busy. However, it is easy to talk with your child about the things that matter most. This makes it easier for us to get on to the important stuff. There will be times when casual conversation is okay, but there will also be occasions when your child requires you to pay close attention.

You need to take the time to explore your child's inner world, even if it isn't obvious to you. This will help them and make them feel better. It will also improve your relationship. Because you truly care, your child will see that you are more understanding of them.

7 Ways to Communicate With Your Children

Here are seven ideas to help you pay more attention to your child when they need it.

1. Listen with your entire body

Your child should have your complete attention at all times. To show your child you are paying attention, turn your face to them. Make eye contact if necessary.

2. Recognize your feelings.

You should pay close attention to how your child uses emotion. Helpful suggestions include making a comment and repeating what they said. This is a sign that you value their opinions and pay attention to them. So, for example, you might ask your child: "Are we unhappy that you won't let us play outside after darkness falls?" These open-ended question allow your child to answer with confirmation or more detail about their feelings. It often leads to more conversation.

3. Respect your child’s emotions.

Empathy is the greatest support we can provide to someone, especially a child. If you acknowledge your child’s emotions, it validates them. This encompasses emotions like wrath, irritation, and disappointment--emotions we frequently categorize as "negative." It is common for children to simply acknowledge their emotions in order to resolve the problem.

Addressing a child's emotions can help increase their awareness and allow them the ability to feel it. It also helps them recognize it in others.

4. Listen more, but fix less.

Even if you think your child is wrong, don't correct them right away. Before you give your answer, be sure to listen. You can take it one step further and ask your child additional questions to find out more about their views. This helps to foster communication and respect your child's feelings. If you're open to listening to their concerns, rather than correcting or judging them, you're more likely to gain cooperation.

5. Look at things through the eyes of your child.

Before you reply, think about what it would be like to be a child. We often assume that young children are able to comprehend the same ideas as adults. This is without taking into consideration their views and thinking methods.

What developmental needs do your child have that are not being met?

You and your husband may decide to take your child out to a movie, but they won't let you leave.

You have two options.

(iii) It's possible for you to get angry at your child and ignore his or her behavior.

(iii). Consider what your child is trying tell you. Is your child's tantrum a cry to you for safety, certainty, support, or something else?

It is easier for you to be logical and patient when you are able to identify the developmental implications of certain actions.

6. Avoid shameful behavior and emphasize good behaviour.

Shaming a kid lowers their value. When a 10-year-old spills his milk at dinner the third time in succession, a parent shouts indignation at him, "You idiot! Can't you be more careful?"

These moments of shame make the child feel inferior over time. Focusing on the behavior can be a better strategy. In similar situations, the father may comment that "it's okay." It's not a problem, let's get a towel out and wipe it clean. You can ask other people to pass your items at the table rather than grab them.

The child doesn't know what to do about their flaws. But with encouragement and guidance, they can learn how to change.

7. Allow your child to come up with unique solutions.

Ask your child about what he would like to see happen, or what he would prefer to change when you are discussing a decision. They will recognize that there can be solutions to every problem.

If they think they can solve the problem, then let them attempt it. Involving children in the process can often make them more motivated to solve problems.

Chapter 7: How To Raise Emotionally-Healthy Children

A parent who cares about and loves their child will have an emotionally healthy child. Certain parenting strategies can help you achieve this and ensure that your child's mental well being is maintained.

One in five children between the ages of 13 and 18 suffers from a major mental disorder. Everybody has a mental disorder nowadays. Even parents can experience depression from time to time. What can you do to support your child's mental health and happiness?

Our children will develop and grow in the right way if we care for them physically and emotionally from the time they are born.

You have a responsibility as a parent to take care of your children from conception. This will help ensure their brain development. It will also benefit their mental health later in the life.

What can you do to support their mental health and satisfy their emotional needs?

As the world moves towards instant gratification, diversions and self-gratification for parents, they are becoming more aware of the content of their cell phones.

Similar to this, parents expose their children to violence by allowing unsupervised screen-time. Read more about the link between screen usage, mental illness and it here.

How can parents help their children to digest the information they have seen? Not at all.

Your children will be influenced by the source - you, the TV, their friends, and their teachers.

Only allow individuals to provide care and protection for them, both spiritually and emotionally.

In a society with rising teen suicide, it is imperative that we take proactive steps to support our children. We must be aware of what our children are exposed to so that they can thrive.

It's becoming more difficult for parents to grasp the needs of their children.

We aren't helpless.

It's crucial to be conscious of the impact we have on our children and make sure that we do all that we can to support them.

7 Steps to Help Your Children Be Emotionally Health

Here are seven ideas to help you raise an emotionally healthy kid.

Keep your Marriage and Yourself Fit

Many agree that mentally well-being is the result of stable families. Abuse, drugs and alcohol are common factors, while mentally sick individuals are the result of unstable homes. It is evident that children are more likely to be healthy if they live in healthy surroundings, with some exceptions.

For the health of your marriage as well as your own personal well-being, it is essential to offer your child the emotional support he or she needs. It's possible to do it if you put your mind to it.

Resolve your marital conflicts. Do your best to invest in your marital relationship and help your child if you have depression or other mental illness.

If you and you spouse are not in a healthy marriage, you will not be able to set a positive example for your child.

To raise emotionally healthy children, it is not a good idea to just bury your head in sand. The most important thing you can do for your kids is to understand their social media habits, current bullying issues and cultural norms.

If you don't have a connection to what they experience at school and with their friends, you won't be able understand how to assist them.

This information will help you stay proactive and avoid reacting to events.

Even though we cannot prevent every possibility, it is possible to help children by becoming more aware of the difficulties they will face as they age.

You should pay more attention to their feelings than to their actions.

Assume your child was playing with their friend at the park. Then another child your child's friend also wants to play.

The new child can make your child feel threatened or withdraw. To express their fear or envy they will act out and make cruel comments to their friend.

You can confront your child's actions and ask them to accept the responsibility for any hurt caused by their friend. Then, you can continue with your previous activities.

What would it be like to do this without knowing?

You would have missed the opportunity to help them recognize their fears and envy.

To achieve this, you need to take them through a process that involves acknowledging and repenting rather than guilt and shame and then ask them later why.

You can tell them that you understand their feelings, and that it's okay for them to feel that way. You should remind them, however, that acting on emotions can lead to both suffering for the friend they care about and for themselves.

You can help them see how envy can affect their emotions, lead into resentment, make their lives miserable.

These are the possibilities we have to grab to teach children how best to handle unpleasant emotions.

These interactions and exchanges will enable you to understand your child fully and show empathy.

It's up to us as individuals to approach them and ask why they do what they do.

Let us suppose that we can understand why they react the way that they do. This will allow us to help them deal with their emotions, and also teach them how we can handle unfavorable situations.

They should be given tasks.

Harvard Research conducted a 75-year-old study that looked at psychological and biological factors during childhood. It found that these factors could predict future health and wellness.

Researchers found that children who have tasks do better in adulthood. According to this article, chores are the best predictor that children will grow up healthy and independent.

You should make it clear that your children can confide to you anything they feel, including the bad.

We cannot expect our children to be up-front and honest with us if they aren't.

Make connections with your children.

Tell your children what your day was like. Ask them about theirs and then share yours. Tell your children about the hard decisions you had at work.

Inform them that your anger at driving caused you to get into an accident and that you have taken responsibility. Allow them to be a part and parcel of your life, so they can benefit from what you have learned.

By modeling healthy behaviors for your child, you will set a good example.

Begin conversations with your children that are emotionally connected and will provide a safe place for them to speak up. With questions like, "If there were a super hero, who would it?," and "Do you think you could tell me anything?" You'll soon be smiling and forming new family bonds. "Do you think you have anything to tell me?"

Encourage regular exercise, and frequent exposure to nature.

The internet and video games can help children build their world. You can teach your child how fascinating and important the world is.

It is possible to incorporate this approach into parenting and teach your child everything from how to make fires, locate treasures and start bug and rock collections, how long and difficult it can take, how to swim in lakes and more.

Accept your faults and say sorry

As a parent, it is essential to show your child that they can feel negative feelings and take responsibility for them.

It is impossible to control the emotions of our children. Your child may feel upset if that's how they feel. Teach your child how they can deal with their emotions.

Your children will be humbled if you apologize.

Humility is one virtue you can instill into your child. It allows people to appreciate others and accept their flaws. It prevents children becoming spoilt brats. You can instill humility in children by taking on the task yourself.

They can learn how they can apologize to others.

In a culture where self-centered, selfish people are the norm, it is possible to make your kids happy, cheerful, satisfied, and appreciative.

Contrary to common belief, children can thrive in life by learning to prioritize all their wants and concerns. Children can learn to care for others and their troubles will seem less serious.

That doesn't mean we should turn a blind eye or ignore their difficulties and struggles. It's about helping your child to see the good in all situations and guiding them towards positive things. Your child can fight against selfish society today by focusing on what they have instead of what they don't.

Chapter 8: Speak Out Change

Begin by becoming aware of your words when you talk about or think about your child. If you use phrases like "You're driving I crazy!" Do you often use phrases like "You drive me crazy!"? Reframe these thoughts by taking a step back. Instead of getting mad at your child for making a mess of their house, think of it as an opportunity that you can teach them how to clean up after themselves. Instead of judging them for not doing their homework on time, ask them how they can help.

You can make an effort to shift your mind when you notice yourself falling into negative thoughts. It might take some time but it will become second instinct. As your relationship with children improves, it will all become worth it.

Here are some useful parenting tips for parents who don't know where they should start:

Begin each day by telling your child what you value about them. It could be something as simple and as straightforward as "I love your sense of humor or "I admire how hardworking"

It is important to praise your child frequently, for both their achievements as well their effort. Saying "Good Job!" is not a good idea. Instead, you can say something like, "I'm so proud about the progress that you've made!" Or "You must've worked hard!"

Negative words such as "no,"" "don’t," or “can’t” should be avoided whenever possible. Instead, think about what your child can accomplish. Instead of saying, "Don’t forget your teeth!”, try saying, "Remember to brush your teeth!" Instead of saying, "Don't forget to brush your teeth!"

Remember to show your child love, affection, and concern. To make your child feel appreciated, hug, kiss, and say affirmations are all good ways to show it.

If you have a positive attitude with your child, it will not only improve their relationship but also help them to see the world in a different way. It's worth a try! You may be surprised by the results.

Happiness comes from Experience, Not Material Goods.

In an effort to make themselves happy, many people purchase items they don't use. The world has become too obsessed with material things. Happiness comes from experiencing life, not material possessions. The best way to be truly happy is to have experiences.

It is vital to remember what will make us happy long term, not what will bring us temporary joy. If you are feeling low, try doing something that will bring back fond memories. These activities will give you a sense satisfaction and contentment beyond what material things can provide.

Doing things together is more enjoyable than working alone, and it will make for better memories. Although it can be nice to own material possessions at times, it's not all that important. There's so much more than what we have in our hands. Enjoy all that life has for you! It's the best thing to make you happy.

If you still aren't convinced, think back to the last trip you took or accomplishment you were proud of. These memories will make you happier than any tangible object. Do not wait! Get out there and have some amazing experiences. You'll be happier.

Be grateful

Although I do not believe humans are born naturally grateful, it is possible to be grateful. It is important to practice gratitude in order to live successful and enjoyable lives. Gratitude is a mental state that can be cultivated through practice.

If you want more joy and to be a better parent and for your children to flourish, start practicing gratitude. Write down five things that you are grateful for each day. You can write five things every day for which you are grateful. They can be substantial ("My health") and small ("The sun is shining") The most important thing is to make time for daily reflection on the good things you have in your life.

It's important to remember that our universe is not all about us. Think about how fortunate you are to be alive today. Millions would trade places with us to have access to the internet, learn more about our lives, and many others. If we are unable to be grateful and express our gratitude, then we should feel ashamed about ourselves.

If we can't find gratitude for our current circumstances we take them as a given. When we take things as granted, we're less likely to be thankful for good things. You become more like a spoiled child who expects everything is going their way and throws tantrums if it does not. On the contrary, grateful people tend to be happier and more content no matter what is going on around them.

Gratitude is a great way to show gratitude for others and for your relationships. Children learn to appreciate others and do better in school. Parents must show gratitude to their children if they want them to be grateful. Let's all make the commitment to be grateful parents and raise grateful kids. It will make our lives happier. Thank you for reading. I hope this was useful.

Chapter 9: Contact Us To Discover Your Strength, And Aliveness.

My parents were so serious and stressed growing up. I wondered how they could not just enjoy life and be more relaxed. It wasn't until my own experience as a parent did I realize how difficult it is for me to find this balance. You are constantly confronted with decisions and challenges that can seem overwhelming as a parent.

It's easy not to see the positives in parenting. If you are positive and open to new opportunities, you will be more successful.

To create the life that you want for your child, it is important to have an open mind and be grateful. If you approach parenting in a respectful manner, you will focus on the good things and bring you joy. You're also more likely to learn from your mistakes to improve your parenting.

Here are some tips to make your parenting experience more positive

Begin each day with gratitude. When you wake up every morning, take some time to appreciate the good things in life. This could include your spouse, children, or any other thing that brings you joy.

Take time to have fun. You need to find ways to have fun while parenting. These activities could include reading with your children or going to a yoga class.

Show gratitude. Thank everyone who supports you. This includes your children, spouse, and friends. A simple "thanks" can go far.

Focus on the now. The best way to reduce stress is by focusing on the now and appreciating the things you have. This does not mean you should forget about your problems. It just means you should stop worrying about the future. Instead, enjoy the moment.

These tips will make parenting easier and more fun for you and the child. A grateful approach to parenting can help you find balance and make the life you dream of.

Ask around

Ask people you trust to share their opinions about your abilities. It might be a good idea to ask others for their views on possible job openings that might fit your strengths and personality. These individuals could be family members or lecturers or close friends. Take an online quiz (such as VIACharacter Strengths Survey) to get a better understanding of your strengths.

This list will help you identify common patterns. Are there any common themes? Perhaps you have a knack for problem-solving, or the ability to work with others. You may be gifted at quickly understanding new concepts. These are just two examples. The possibilities for many others are endless. The most important thing is to start understanding what makes you tick. Knowing your strengths makes it much easier to identify possible career paths.

But it isn't enough to know your strengths. You need to also be able and willing to share them. These strengths must be clearly articulated to show why they would make you an effective candidate for a specific job. This skill is not easy for everyone, but it is one that can be taught with practice. Next time you have a conversation, be sure to include your strengths. To illustrate, if you are trying to sell your problem-solving abilities, you might say, “I'm skilled at finding creative solutions to difficult issues.” Once you understand your strengths, and can communicate them to others, you'll be better equipped to find the right job.

Find out your strengths as a person and put them to work for you and your child.

There are many personality strengths that we all share. Some are more outgoing and others more reflective. No matter your personality strengths or weaknesses, you can still create a life with your child that is meaningful and loving.

Here are some suggestions on how to harness your strengths as a personality to create the life of your dreams.

You might be naturally introverted. Spend some time each day reflecting upon what you are grateful to your child. This will help you see your child in a positive light and allow you to concentrate on their positive attributes.

If you're outgoing and naturally outgoing then spend time with your child each day. This could be done through play, conversation or quality time. This will deepen your connection and understanding of each other.

No matter what personality you have, remember to be kind and accept your child no matter what. This will provide a foundation for a happy and healthy marriage.

If you can understand and appreciate your strengths, it will be easier to see how your child's strengths complement them. This will allow you to leverage your strengths and create a positive partnership with your child.

Numerous online quizzes and assessments will help you discover your personality strengths. Your Strengths can be used to guide your parenting.

Look for patterns

Take note of what works and make an effort to do more. Try to avoid negativity and negative habits, as well as things that don't work. Talk to people who have lived the life you dreamed with their children. Let go of what isn't working, and be grateful for what is.

The effort required to build the life you desire with your child is hard work. But the rewards will be well worth it. Appreciative thinking will help you get there. It's important to take time to evaluate what's working and to plan for more of the things that work. You've got this!

Chapter 10: Determining Your Child's Strengths And Aliveness.

We can begin to see the potential for a warm, respectful relationship with our children if we ask ourselves what most we appreciate about them. This doesn't necessarily mean that we have to ignore their negative behaviors or overlook them. However, it does allow us to see ourselves and them in a new light full of possibility and hope.

If we can focus on the things we love, it is easier to see potential in our children. It is possible to discover hidden talents and other forms of aliveness we didn't even know existed. Our appreciation will help our children blossom as they begin to see the best in us. It's an amazing feedback loop that can greatly affect both the parent as well as the child.

To help our children discover their strengths and to be respectful parents, we can use respectful parenting. It's possible to help your children build their confidence and competence by encouraging them and taking an active interest in what they are good at. They naturally become more aware of their gifts and are more appreciative of others.

A grateful mindset creates a trusting and safe environment. Children who feel valued, respected, and loved are more likely to be open to new experiences and take risks. As they learn how to communicate their needs and desires, they also learn to understand and empathize.

Each child is born with unique talents and flaws. It's normal to be focused on the negative aspects of your child's life and areas where they can make improvements. It is also important to recognize your child’s strengths. It will help you improve your child’s self-awareness. You can also use your strengths to help you work through more difficult areas. Children are more likely be persistent when they are doing something they enjoy.

It can be difficult for us to shift our focus from the wrong to right. However, respectful parenting has many benefits. They will begin to see the best and become more aware of the possibilities in the world around them. Do it now and you will see a change in your relationship to your child.

You should consider different strengths.

There are many strengths. They can be visible or hidden, large or small. You can use the checklist to help identify strengths, but don’t get too focused on thinking your child must have them all. Look for the ones that appeal to you and focus your attention on them.

Your child's potential strengths could be:

* Learning well in school

* Being a good friend

* Being creative

* Playing sport

* Making people smile

* Helping others

* Being sincere

* Positivity

Whatever your child’s strengths, look for ways to help them develop. Recognizing your child's strengths, like all things in life, will help you feel better and motivate them to keep using them. Both of you will live a happier and more fulfilling life. Thank you for reading. I hope you found it useful.

You should consider different types of strengths.

It doesn't matter what size or scope of your family, strengths can be found no matter where you look. This checklist will help you identify your child's strengths so you can begin practicing respectful parenting right away.

Begin by taking inventory of your child’s strengths and talents. If your child struggles in school, you should look for signs that they have intelligence or talent in other areas, such as music, art or socializing with friends. It's crucial to place importance on their unique talents, rather than worrying about what they may not have.

Next, take an active part in your child's hobbies and lives. See their excitement and take an interest. This will help them feel more confident and bond with you on a deeper level.

Final thoughts: Celebrate your child's achievements, large or small. Even a simple, "good job" is enough to get the job done. But you might consider going above and beyond by giving your child a treat or activity. This will make them feel proud of their accomplishments, and encourage them towards excellence.

You can help your child find their strengths.

Your child can make a "strengths-chain" to visualize their strengths, or an "accomplishmentsbox" to track their successes. This will help them feel good about themselves.

The online assessment is free and can help you find your child's strengths. You will receive tailored support recommendations based on your child's individual needs, interests, resilience, and other factors.

Your child will soon be able to appreciate the gifts they have and use these to make their lives more fulfilling. You will be amazed at the impact gratitude can make on your child's life.

Note the strengths and achievements of your child.

Keep an eye on your child. Note the achievements (both small and big) and the talents that have helped them achieve them. It is also helpful to notice problems. It's a lovely way to say, “Here's the thing I saw.” I'm proud to say that you did a wonderful job. This is one Appreciative Parenting activity.

It can be hard to both be critical and open-minded at the same moment. You will be able to see your child in a more positive light if you focus on their successes. With this attitude of positivity, it is possible to have deeper conversations with your child about the things they do well and the areas where they need improvement. These conversations will be much more productive than if only you point out what your kid is doing wrong.

It is important not to pretend that everything is perfect. Your goal is to see the good in children so that they can become their best selves. Your parenting will become more efficient if you concentrate on the positive.

Next time you feel angry with your child, try taking a step back to look at things from an appreciation perspective. This may be the key to creating the life you want for your child.

It's easy to get distracted by parenting difficulties and forget the bigger picture. It is possible to see our children for the unique individual they are by taking a step back and being appreciative. It is possible to help your children be their best selves when we approach them with appreciation. Be grateful the next time your child is frustrated. You may be able to make the changes you want in your relationship with your child.

Imagine your preferred future.

If you spend the time to visualize your dream future with your child, it opens you up to new possibilities. What do you envision your ideal future looking like? What kind of relationship will you have with your child? How would you like them to feel about their self?

It can be very powerful if you take notes or share your answers with someone else. If you have a vision you can look back to, it will keep you motivated and can even remind you why you did all of this hard work.

Practice balance.

Good planning will ensure that we don't run out tomorrow morning. It is important to make smart decisions today in order to live every day to its fullest. Family ties and making a living are balanced. Relationships are managed to keep up with tomorrow's demands. That equilibrium is not there looking for anyone, so it will make all of the difference.

Appreciative Inquiry helps us to see that our children have always been worthy of our gratitude, no matter how they behave. A whole new world opens up when we focus on what we are grateful to for, for our children and ourselves.

We are more likely than not to see the negative side of things if we keep our eyes on the positive. We can look at our children's tantrums in the middle grocery store and realize that they are only trying to express their emotions. This does not mean that we must allow them to be this way all the times, but it does allow us to respond constructively and usefully rather than being harsh and destructive.

Take a moment to reflect on the situation next time you get frustrated with your child. You may be surprised at the difference in your feelings and how much easier it is to parent.

When my son was just two years old, he experienced a period where he would throw tantrums every time we went to the grocery shop. It was frustrating and I wondered why I even wanted to have children. I was reminded of the importance of respectful parenting and decided that I would try to change my perspective.

I started to notice all the blessings I had, even when there were tantrums. I was thankful to my son's energy and passion, his willingness to speak his mind, and the fact he was still struggling to understand how to communicate. This helped me see the situation in a constructive and helpful light, and eventually the tantrums disappeared.

Spend less than your monthly earnings.

This simple rule can have far-reaching effects. After digging out the sand, more than half is redeposited. Start by restoring your financial health. Pay your debt. Keep in mind that your debt will cost you more interest than your savings. Third, you should save at minimum ten per cent of your income. The sooner you begin saving, the longer your money must grow.

Fourth, you should invest your savings smartly. Investing allows you to make your money work hard for you. When done correctly, investing is a way to secure a comfortable retirement. It can help pay college tuition and even fund other important goals such buying a home or starting businesses. You should be aware of the risks involved in investing.

Fifth, you can give yourself permission for some of the hard-earned dollars to be spent on things that make your happy. Isn't this what true happiness is all about? Make sure you keep your spending under control so you don't go back to debt.

Chapter 11: Recognizing Self Care's Importance

Take care of your own health and well-being as a parent. This includes making time for hobbies, interests, or friendships. While it might seem selfish, this is one of most selfless things you could do. By taking care of yourself, you're setting an example of healthy behavior for your kids. It's also a way to say "My needs matter too!"

This does not mean you have to prioritize your child. This doesn't mean you have to neglect yourself. Regular self-care can help you be a better parent. It will reduce stress, increase patience, and improve your mood.

You might feel stressed or overwhelmed if you take a step back. Then ask yourself what you need. This could be as simple as walking around your block or reading a favorite book. You might consider signing up for yoga classes or going on a weekend escape with friends. Whatever your choice, ensure you make time every week for yourself. It will pay off in the long term for your family.

Parents know this rule well. Raising children can be a 24-hour job that requires almost constant sacrifices of time, energy, and effort. Parents may feel overwhelmed by their children's egocentricity, which can cause them to try to satisfy all of their needs. The cycle of letting children control our lives only makes it worse.

Everyone needs balance in their lives. It doesn't matter if we binge watch, eat high-quality food, or simply listen to music, we all need some downtime. Children often believe that they must always be available for their parents. It is crucial that we understand what our requirements are and ensure that they are met.

Keep in mind that even if your child's schedule is causing you stress, you still matter. You are vital in this equation, so you have to make sure that you take care of yourself as well your children. It doesn't mean that you have to be available for every request of your child 24 hours a night, seven days a semaine. Although you are always available for emergency situations, this does not mean that you will be available to every child's request. You might be limited in the amount of time you have or how long you'll be available for their activities.

This is often a sign that one is selfish for taking time for oneself. This mindset causes individuals to give everything they have until they are bitter or resentful. At this point, people can become irritable, sour, or lose interest in parenting. You will never be able to recharge the batteries if all you do is give. Children often believe it's all in their hands. Because they are developmentally unable to understand the limits of your energy or attention, children often believe that it's all about them.

It's not selfish for you to care for your own needs. In fact, it is the most selfless thing you as a parent can do. If you take care for yourself, you set a good example and show your children that you value their needs. This does not mean you have to prioritize your child, but it does suggest that you don't feel guilty about taking time for yourself every now and again. Regular self-care can help you be a better parent. It can reduce stress, improve patience, and boost your mood. You don't have to feel stressed out or overwhelmed if you are feeling burnt out. Take a step back, and think about what you need to do for yourself. Perhaps it is as simple as taking time to read or walk around your block. You might also consider signing up for yoga classes or planning a weekend getaway with your friends. Whatever your choice, ensure you make time every week for yourself. It will pay off in the long term for your family.

Make time for friends and family

Even though it's important, self-care can be difficult when you don’t have time to see family members and friends as they are.

It is a great way to plan for a future event (which can also be a helpful self-care technique). Then, you will find that social activities are a great way to boost your psychological well-being. You can make it a priority in your schedule to meet with friends and family regularly, even if you don't have the time. It can be much easier than you realize, and your children may also benefit.

Schedule time for social activities can boost your psychological well-being. It will also improve your parenting skills. You and your child will both benefit from a happier, more involved parent. Remember to schedule in some "me time" with your family and friends.

It can seem daunting to find the time to take care of yourself when you are already busy taking care your little one(s). But it is worth remembering that investing in your happiness will make you a better parent. You are the best version you can be for your children.

Don't hesitate to reach out and make a friend, join a book club, or enroll in a yoga class. Your family, and you, will be so glad that you did.

Give yourself time to be alone

Many parents find that the only place they feel alone is in the bathroom. You need to be able to calm down and not get too excited. A little bit of solitude can make it easier to wind down. It doesn't matter if you have to wait until your child falls asleep, or until someone is there to look after your kid, you can take some time alone to recharge your batteries and be the best person for your family.

You can be grateful for what you have. When you are not at your best it will be difficult to see the good and appreciate the positives in others. By taking time to yourself, you can return home feeling rejuvenated and ready to provide your full attention to your loved ones. You can also avoid burnout by giving yourself some "me-time". It's a good idea to put yourself first from time to time - it will pay off for you and your family long term!

Appreciative parenting has the potential to change our relationship with our kids and our parenting style. It's an attitude that focuses on the positive. When we look at our children and their behavior with an appreciation lens, we can see the best possible in every situation. With this perspective, we can better parent with intention.

Enhance Communication With Your Child

If you keep your eyes on the positive, it will help your child feel valued. Appreciative attitude can improve communication with your children. This attitude will allow you to see the best in your child and help you work together to achieve the life you want.

Know that every interaction you have with your child is a form or communication. It goes far beyond words. The way that you sound, the way your eyes look, and even the actions you take, all send messages to your child. Your example of how you interact with other people will be set by the way you communicate with them. It can also influence their emotional development, and the kinds of relationships they develop later on in life. So make sure your communication is positive.

Active listening

Active listening can help children feel valued and heard. Your child may appreciate your attention and show you care by smiling and nodding. You will be more secure and closer to your child if you keep your eyes on them as they talk to each other. Ask them questions like, "What?" "why?" "Why?" & "How?" It will show that you are paying attention to what they have said. You can see their facial expressions but not your reaction. This helps them communicate and learn how to tell stories.

It also shows that your child is interested in you and their thoughts. Children are more likely to feel valued and to be positive about you when they feel it. To illustrate, if your child is coming home from school and tells us about their day. Instead of interrupting them or asking questions, just say "it sounds like it was a great day!" This will let your child know that you appreciate their successes and would love to hear about their day. Appreciative parenting means listening to your child and letting them know you value what they have said. You will be amazed at the impact these tips have on your relationship with your child.

Respectful parenting involves active listening. If we listen to our children actively, it shows them that we value and respect them. This builds trust and respect and helps you communicate well. These tips will make a huge difference in the way you communicate with your children.

Reflective listening

It is also a great way of showing your child you care about their feelings by being a mirror. In a different language, repeat what your child says to you. To illustrate, if your child states, "I'm tired of playing with Marco anymore", you might ask softly, without judging, and say, "You aren't playing with your friend anymore?" What has happened?

In many cases, adults are surprised at how much they have and the child feels heard.

This approach is also useful in arguments. Listening to the other person when you are defensive can be very difficult. You can diffuse tension by taking a step back to listen to what they are saying and learn more about their viewpoint. Although you may not agree with their views, you will at least be able to see the bigger picture.

Some people find that it is easier to imagine holding a cup while listening. The cup represents the person's feelings. While speaking, the listener fills it up and pours any remaining water over the sides. This analogy reminds that it is important to not interrupt or judge the person as they speak. It also reminds you that we shouldn't try to solve someone's problems, but instead be there for their needs.

It is difficult to listen to someone when you are defensive. You can diffuse tension by taking a step back to listen to what they are saying and learn more about their viewpoint. Although you may not agree with their views, you can at least see where they are coming.

Chapter 12: The Power To Influence Kids' Emotions Is Rapidly Slipping Away

This article will explain how emotional self regulation develops and how parents can help their children learn this important skill.

What is emotional regulation?

Emotional regulation is also known as self-regulation. This refers to the ability of one to regulate and monitor which emotions are present and how they are expressed.

In child development, self-regulation is a crucial milestone. The foundations for this skill are laid in childhood.

A child's ability to regulate their emotions can impact their family, peers, academic performance and long-term mental well-being. This will affect their ability and potential to thrive within a complex world.

4 children look up at the heavens and laugh - What is Emotional regulation in child development?

RELATIONSHIPS TO FAMILY AND PEERS

A child with poor emotional regulation skills may throw tantrums and put a strain on parent-child relationships. This can lead to a downward spiral and affect the household's overall climate.

The same goes for friendships. Kids who struggle to control their emotions have lower social skills. They have a harder job keeping and making friends. They may exhibit aggressive behaviors, such as anger, withdrawal and anxiety.

All this can lead to further problems: Children who aren't liked by their peers are more likely drop out of school and become addicted to drugs or have other antisocial behaviors. Bullying can also be more likely for those who are withdrawing and rejected by their peers.

PERFORMANCE, SUCCESS

In contrast, emotional regulation in children is not only positive for relationships but also a strong predictor and predictor of academic success.

Emotion management is a skill that allows students to be more focused on the exam and not worry about their anxiety.

Self-regulation helps students pay more attention, solve problems faster, and is better for tasks that involve inhibition, delayed gratification, and long-term goals.

This effect lasts throughout one's life. Unable to manage emotions properly can have lower job satisfaction, mental health and overall well-being.

RESILIENCE, MENTAL HEALTH

Children who have learned to regulate emotions can better manage trauma or adverse events.

Many childhood disorders can be closely linked to emotional regulation.

Children with emotional dysregulation are more susceptible to developing future psychopathology. A child with future psychopathology is also at greater risk.

This is why experts consider emotions regulation and self-regulation essential skills that children should develop.

Check out this video from The Center on the Developing Child Harvard University.

Harvard Video: Emotional Self Regulation in Children

How does emotional regulation develop in children?

How do children learn these crucial skills? And what can we do to support them as parents?

Let's answer these questions by looking at the definition of emotional regulation for children.

Notice: Self-regulation is about being aware of, monitoring, and recognizing different emotions - and adapting them for each situation.

This doesn't mean you have to suppress your negative feelings and increase your positive ones. A self-regulation process that involves suppressing negative feelings or forcing ourselves not too express them isn't effective.

IS IT EASIER TO LEARN EMOTIONAL REGULATION FOR SOME CHILDREN THAN OTHERS.

It doesn't make sense that some kids are more difficult at emotional regulation than others.

Researchers discovered that some babies' temperaments are naturally more capable than others of self-regulation6.

Although genetics are important in some cases, it's just as important that a child is raised in a nurturing environment.

The ability to self-regulate does not come in stone. Children can learn to manage their emotions, provided they have the right environment.

Study in a Romanian foster home illustrates the importance environment. In this study, orphans were randomly assigned foster homes with high quality care. Others remained in the orphanage. The adoption children showed significant improvements in emotional regulation compared to those who stayed7.

Also, see: How Coregulation Converts to Self-Regulation in Children

Cartoon of a child and his brain being repaired by workers at a construction site - Emotional intelligence

WHY IS CHILDHOODLIFE IMPORTANT IN LEARNING SELF - REGULATIONSKILLS

The brains of babies when they are born are not fully developed. Our brains are still developing. It's a little like building a house.

A house's architectural blueprint may help it shape but the end result will depend on whether the house is made out of straw, wood, or Brick.

Genetics also determine the basic blueprint for a child's brain growth, but life experiences, like those of the house's builders, can greatly influence the outcome8.

As it's simpler to affect a house during its construction than later, so too can humans learn some skills easier or more efficiently during certain periods of their lives. These ideal times are called critical and sensitive periods.

After the difficult period of learning a skill, the ability to become proficient gradually decreases.

The ability to learn a new skill is still possible, but it may take longer or be less effective.

Studies have shown that the best time to learn a second tongue and become truly bilingual is before puberty.

Romanian orphanage experiment: Orphans adopted by foster homes before the age 2 developed emotional regulation skills that were comparable to children who had never been institutionalized.

Children between the ages 2 and 3 are believed to have reached their sensitive phase of emotional self regulation. Science has proven that early childhood experiences have a profound impact on emotional self-regulation.

This does not mean that kids will no longer be able to learn self regulation once they are older. It just means that it will prove more difficult, and will require more patience and time.

It's much better to do it right when your children are young than to fix it later.

Don't be discouraged if your child is an older person. It's never too soon to teach children self-regulation. Start now! The sooner you start, the better.

But, this does not mean that the learning process to self-regulate by the age of 2 is complete. The brain development of a child is not complete until his/her twenties.

Diagram of Sympathetic Division, Parasympathetic Division.

PARENTS ARE ESSENTIAL IN HELPING CHILDREN ABUSE EMOTION REGULATION SKILLS

Our nervous systems are composed of two components that regulate our brains.

The "gas pedal" is an emergency response or quick-response mechanism. It activates the body's fight/flight response.

This system is similar to the accelerator in a car's engine. This system allows the body to move faster when activated. It speeds up our heart rate and shuts down digestion.

This is when the baby or child's emotions get out of control and their system kicks into high gear. This is often called the emotional brain, or downstairs brain taking control.

The "brake" is second. This is a calming, or dampening, part of our brain.

The maturation and development of the infant's brake system are key factors in their ability to regulate their emotions.

This calmer part of our nervous can counter "high speed" effects caused by fight-or-flight. It's essential in controlling our bodily function and emotional well being. This calming mechanism is controlled by the cognitive (or the upstairs), brain.

When these systems work together, our bodies are able to function well and our emotions are under control.

To restore equilibrium to systems that are out of balance, it is important to use self-regulation techniques.

Because the human survival of the fight-or flee response is so important, it's no surprise that the "gas pump" begins before birth. Each parent is aware that newborns can be sufficiently alerted to parents' needs or danger by crying.

The "brakes", however, are not as developed at birth. The infants only have a limited amount of self-regulation abilities such as thumb sucking or visual avoidance. They are unable to self-soothe if they are stressed out or if they don't get the message.

A stress hormone can be released from the "gas pedal" to stop the "brake" from being activated.

Baby's uncontrollable crying is a sign that they are driving an emotionally runaway car. Our role as parents is to help our children manage their emotions. Their nervous systems may not be able to handle the task.

How to help your child manage their emotions

While there are many factors that can influence a child's ability or inability to regulate, like teachers, schools. neighborhoods. peers. culture. and genetics. Parents and families play an important role.

Let's consider the main factors that influence children’s ability to self regulate their emotions.

Baby rides on dad's shoulder

Learner who is self-motivated

Have trouble motivating your child? Take a look at:

HOW TO MOTIVATE KIDS

1. PARENTS MODELING EMOTION - REGULATINGSKILLS

Since long, modeling has been recognized as an important tool for children to learn. Children watch their parents closely and begin to imitate them.

Their parents' ability practice self-regulation is one of the first examples that children see in relation to emotion.

The correct response in different situations is what kids learn. They can see their parents struggle to control intense emotions and impulses11.

Research shows that children whose parents have difficulty with emotional regulation are more susceptible to developing dysregulation12.

If a parent reacts by screaming, screaming, or shouting whenever something goes wrong, then the child will learn to be reactive and misbehave if things don't go as planned.

When a parent is calm, thinks critically and solves problems, the child is more likely not to get upset and to look for solutions. The stronger the imitation effect13, the younger the child.

Aside from active observation, children also learn via emotional contagion. Children unconsciously sense emotions in their parents and respond with the same feelings14.

Kids can become angry when their parents frown, raise the volume, or make angry gestures. Kids will also raise their volume if their parents shout.

Teaching children self-regulation through modeling behavior is the best way to do it. Parents are the ones who influence children's emotional regulation.

For children who aren't able to find a good role model, emotional regulation activities and tools should be used only as a last resort or supplement. These tools should not be substituted for parental modeling.

As the child gets older peer influence joins parental influence. Older kids learn self-regulation from watching and copying their peers.

The quality of the parent/adolescent relationship is still a major factor in the adolescent's selfregulation15.

Parents can help kids develop effective emotional control.

You can work with your therapist to learn better ways to regulate your emotions.

For children, model positive emotions for them and adaptive emotion regulation

Encourage children to be in a positive and self-regulating environment.

2. PARENTS SHOULD CHOOSE A RESPONSIVE WARMING AND ACCEPTING PARENTING STATEMENT

Accepting, loving, and responsive parenting can help children social-emotional development as well as behavioral control.

If parents are responsive, children associate them as comfort and relief from stress.

Research shows that babies who hear their parents crying will stop crying if they are near them.

If the parent fails to offer comfort, the child will go back to their distressed state16. Children of responsive parents have greater access to regulatory skills.

Important is the belief of parents in emotion management.

People who accept, validate, and empathize positively with their children's feelings are more likely to have a positive effect on them. They can teach children emotional awareness by helping them to communicate how they feel and encouraging problem solving.

Parents who are critical or dismissive of emotions, particularly negative, can lead to children developing destructive emotional regulation strategies17.

These parents often feel uncomfortable expressing emotions, and they tend to coach their kids to suppress those feelings.

Parents who punish or react negatively to their children's emotions can make them more stressed, triggering their "fight/flight" nervous systems and making it more difficult for them to calm themselves down.

Sometimes, this can appear like the child is being more stubborn, but their system may be over-stimulated. If a child is having a meltdown, telling them to "calm Down" or threatening to punish them may cause their systems to be over-stimulated.

These children tend to have lower self-regulation skills and are less able to manage a stressed-out system. The opposite of emotional regulation is teaching it through punishment.

Some parents take the sweeping-under-the-rug approach when it comes to negative emotions. They believe that if they can't see it or don't want it to exist, then it won't exist.

Unfortunately, emotions don’t work in this way. Children whose parents ignore their emotions and don't talk to them in a supportive manner are less capable of managing their own emotions well.

This parenting approach is a great way to teach kids self-regulation.

They should be open and accepting of their child's emotions.

Talk about emotions

Accept, support, show empathy, and validate their negative emotions

Be patient

Do not dismiss, demoralize, punish, or ignore your child's emotions.

Mom and brother to tickle girl – Emotion regulation activity that you can use the next time you want to improve your interpersonal skills

3. FOSTERING A POSITIVE, EMOTIONAL CLIMATE WITH THE FAMILY

A child's self-regulation ability can be predicted by the environment around them20.

Factors that can affect the emotional climate are the parents' relationships, their personalities and parenting styles, as well as sibling relationships and family beliefs about how to express feelings.

Children feel comfortable and accepted when their emotions are positive, consistent, and responsive.

When the emotional climate in a school is negative, coercive or unpredictable, children tend to be more reactive, and insecure.

Positive emotions from parents can create a positive environment.

Parents who display negative emotions, like anger, hostility or sadness, frequently or excessively, are a problem for their children's self-regulation.

The most common reason for a dysfunctional family is marital violence. These children are taught non-constructive techniques to manage their emotions and interpersonal conflicts. These children are less likely21 to develop social competency.

Parents can make a positive atmosphere in the home by creating a family culture.

Expressions of genuine positive emotions

Ask for help in dealing with marital disputes or other negative members of the family

Work to improve parent-child relationships as well as relationships between siblings

4.GROWNUPS TEACHINGSELF REGULATING SKILLS and TECHNIQUES

So far we have covered three different methods that parents can help their kids self regulate. If you think it seems like parents must do more than just the kids to control their emotions, then you are correct.

To learn self-regulation, young kids rely on adults. As they age, their executive functions become more important22. Parents can help their children learn self-help skills.

James Gross and collaborators proposed a process model of emotion regulation. It consists of five stages for emotion generation23. You can use different self-regulation strategies to regulate your emotions at each stage.

Stage 1: Situation Selection. This stage involves selecting the best situation for you based on your likely emotional impact.

Stage 2: Environment Modification - Modifying the environmental conditions to alter their emotional impact.

Stage 3 - Attentional Deployment is a redirection of attention to a situation that can influence one's emotions.

Stage 4 - Cognitive Change – Evaluating the situation in order alter its emotional significance.

Stage 5 Response Modulation: Influencing emotional tendencies or reactions when they arise.

Because children are less capable of changing their environment or avoiding it, the majority of coping strategies for children address these three stages. They are less likely to be able to connect emotion and circumstance.

Here are some tips for parents to teach older children.

Stage 3: Redirect attention (e.g. Here's a red bunny!

Stage 4 - Reappraisal via reframing situation25 You can transform this into a rocket

Stage 5: Coping skills (e.g. biofeedback26. count to 10, deep breaths, and breathing exercises

5. SELF-CARE

For adolescents and teenagers aged over 18, self-care is vital in helping them to manage their emotions. You can improve self-care by engaging in the following activities:

Swimming, running, and any other aerobic activity can be done.

Mindfulness practice27 like meditation and yoga

Good sleep hygiene and adequate rest are key to good health.

Relaxation treatments like listening to music

Final thoughts on emotional regulation in children

If you feel that the information on teaching children self-regulation is overwhelming, it is. It is a reminder about the role of parents in shaping the futures of our children.

We all have our limitations. Insisting on perfection may lead to stress and negativity.

All we have to do is keep improving our emotional skills and creating a supportive atmosphere. It's never too soon to start.

You can take deep breaths and be present for yourself and your family. It's definitely worth it.

This step-by–step guide provides more guidance on how to calm tantrums.

Calm the Tantrums ebook

Is your child having trumping problems?

Temper tantrums can occur at any age, not just toddlers. It is possible for school-age children to have difficulty controlling their emotions. (Even adults throw tantrums sometimes!)

Calm The Tantrums offers great tips and a step by step plan.

It provides the steps necessary to calm toddler tantrums.

This guide covers the top three methods to prevent toddler tantrums, strategies for parents to remain calm, and the best ways to handle hitting.

If you are able to teach your children how to regulate their emotions, you can create a peaceful and happy home.

Chapter 13: The Dangers Of Kids' Emotions

Children as young as one began to express emotions. You started to see it in them. You remember when you said, "Ouchie", and he turned his head as if to laugh at the sight of that toy car. That's quite a feeling! Jaime Gleicher LMSW, a behavioral therapist at Hartstein Psychological Services Center (New York City), says that parents implicitly explain, illustrate and show their children why they shouldn't behave in a certain manner.

We often don't spend the same effort to give those kinds of emotional clues as school-aged children. She says, "If all you do is tell your child that she has to go to her place when she misbehaves then you are losing the opportunity to talk to her about why and how she feels." These small gestures can help you open the door for dialogue with your child to understand the complexity of emotions.

"A school course is not available to teach emotions. But, it's important to establish and increase your child's emotional intelligence. Gleicher agrees that learning emotions is just as important as learning numbers, letters, or color sorting. The purpose of emotions is to help us understand the world around us.

Based upon previous experiences, emotions provide quick insight to use as a means of making sense of what's happening around us.

RELATED! How to help your preschooler handle emotions and avoid outbursts

While you're young, there are no previous experiences that you can draw on. Instead, your responses to emotions will depend solely on how you feel. It's up the caregiver or parent of the child to show them how to recognize, label their emotions, interpret and apply them. Gleicher argues that it will give children a new vocabulary for self expression. This language is not designed to make people feel numb, harmed, suppressed, or pushed down. It helps them understand what they are feeling. Gleicher states, "The best gift that you can give your kids, it is the ability of feeling, understanding, and deal with emotions. It will be their key to resilience in later life."

You don't need to try and describe every emotion for your child. Start with the most important. You will find the most common, complex emotions from which all other emotions are derived and how you can communicate them to your children.

How to Teach Mindfulness To Your Kids

Anger is a feeling of anger, dissatisfaction and discontent. A child who is upset by a playmate stealing their toy can quickly become angry. Their fight or flight reflexes may be stimulated. Your child will react to stimuli which cause him pain or displeasure, such as throwing a tantrum, striking, or doing anything wrong.

Jaclyn Schlisky is a licensed psychologist in Long Island. It is important to discuss your child's behavior (the anger or hostility that he is expressing) while it is happening.

Identify the feeling. It's important not to use decisive words such "I see" instead of words like "It look like" or even "It appears." Gleicher says you should not put any particular words on an event that could invalidate your child’s emotions. Gleicher explains that if the youngster doesn't feel sad or scared, it's okay to use these words. Gleicher states, "It gives youngster the opportunity to correct parents if this isn't true."

Explain the feeling. Say "Sometimes things don’t go the way that we want them to, and that makes it sad and frustrating." You can then teach your youngster how to express these sensations. Practice expressing your feelings with your youngster by saying "I don’t love when you yank a toys out of my hands." Gleicher suggests that unpleasant behaviors, such as screaming, hitting, and sobbing while feeling angry, are a sign of an underlying emotion that hasn't been managed or healed. Meltdowns are an emotion that cannot be understood. Your kid will need you to communicate what they feel since they may not be able. This is called improving the emotional language of your child.

She says, "They need a word to identify with the sensation so that they can use their language to express rather than react." Gleicher encourages parents to ask their children how they feel if their child throws a tantrum, strikes out, or does any other unacceptable behavior. By asking your child how they feel, they will learn that anger can lead them to strike and that they have the option of expressing it in different ways. "The message should be that you can feel emotions and that they are temporary, this is OK. You can also do it on the opposite end of the spectrum. How do YOU feel?"

What can you do to make it easier? Point out emotion in others. Ask your kids how they think the character feels when you are reading or watching movies. Gleicher agrees, "This not only builds emotional vocabulary but also teaches empathy, which is the act of putting yourself in other people's shoes."

6 Mindfulness Activities Families Can Do

Sadness

For your children, the feeling of being lost, grieved, or letdown is very important. Sadness could be caused by your child feeling scared, or when someone else does or says something terrible to him. Sadness may result from the loss of a loved one (either through death or distance), or through having to deal with difficult emotions (e.g. hearing or seeing your parents argue). Sadness can also come from disappointment, such the closing of schools because of the coronavirus virus outbreak or a missed play date.

Identify the feeling. Dr. Shlisky suggests that kids who feel upset will not only feel sad, but also think sad and behave sad. Your child's most obvious sign is tears. However, they may also show melancholy other than tears.

"By the point they reach 1, newborns are able to recognize that their parents can help control their emotions. They cry and you run. Dr. Shlisky says that toddlers start to understand the connection between certain emotions and specific events as they get older. Without understanding the root causes of melancholy, sadness can turn into anger and eventually lead to meltdowns. If your child cries every time you try to console them, you are just trying to put a bandage on a problem instead of solving the root cause. Dr. Shlisky explains that children need the skills to express "I feel sorry ..."" because otherwise they might learn that their emotions may be muffled, and they won't be able define the root causes of their grief.

Explain the sensation.

They may be able to relate to you about a similar loss they have suffered. Be open about how unhappy and how you cried. Talk about how you were able to overcome your sorrowful emotions. To demonstrate that things will be okay, parents are often strong for their children. But it is healthy for children to watch adults show proper emotion. It is acceptable to say that "Daddy is sad, too." Dr. Shlisky says that it is okay to say, "Daddy is unhappy too."

How to make things simpler: Do not suggest "use my words" when your child is unhappy. It is unfair when the child is still learning how the body and mind interact with each other. Gleicher states, "I recommend that parents create an emotions chart using Emojis that kids love and then use it as a way to help your kids understand how facial expressions can link to feelings." You can even point to the phrase if the child can't name the sensation.

Fear

Children are not naturally afraid, but fear is a result of anxiety and concern. Gleicher explained that children who feel afraid are more likely to be aware of risks. Some concerns are natural. Many children fear strangers, the dark and are isolated from their families. Not everyone can have happy days. Your child could have witnessed something or heard someone say something, or been in an actual-life situation that scared them, such as a car accident.

Identify the feeling. Dr. Shlisky recommends Dr. Shlisky to calmly and factually deliver the message so that your youngster feels at ease.

Explain the feeling. You might say something similar ("I feel that too"), and then ask your child questions. You don't have to know the answer. It's great for your child to know that you will search methods to find out more and then return to them with an answer. Sometimes all it takes to help your child is to allow him or her to express his thoughts. She says that sometimes children need to talk to us because the things are too important for them to hold on to. Giving him the assurance that there is always someone to listen, and that there is always an open door for him, might provide the comfort he requires.

How to make things more manageable: Children often have difficulty communicating the cause of their anxiety to their parents. Telling stories, imagining events, or reading books about difficult situations can help them overcome their fears. Experts recommend reading to children novels such as Wemberly Worried, The Color Monster, and Wemberly Scared.

Jealousy

Francyne Zelter, Psy.D., New York psychologist says that envy is a green-eyed monster. It can take over and it shows up in toddlers as young at 3 months. It's a feeling that is easy to feel and expresses itself easily. A mom might hug a strangers baby, or gift her brother with goodies on his birthday. However the idea of envy is difficult to describe. It may be feelings or thoughts of uneasiness or anxiety or worry about relative safety and assets. However, it may also include the sensations of inadequacy. Feelings of envy usually stem from an individual's inability to fulfill their needs. Dr. Zeltser says it may be due to lack of trust or insecurity.

Identify the feeling. Jealousy and jealousy are very similar. But envy is a desire for something you have never had. And jealousy is a fear of losing what you have, or at least the thought of having.

Material jealousy ("I want her stuff") begins at the age of toddlerhood. "Toddlers are not afraid to grab toys from their friends. Dr. Zeltser said that although children learn society standards and are enrolled in school, they tend to stop taking what they want. However, it doesn't stop them being envious of the toys their peers have. Your family's non-monetary wealth is worth more than material possessions. Flexible work hours might mean you can spend more time with your family. So that you don't feel inadequate, turn the narrative around to make sure you feel secure.

5 Mindfulness and Meditating Apps for Kids

You might also feel social jealousy if you don't invite your daughter to a sleepover. Dr. Zeltser explains that some youngsters are able to see fairness as a way of generating inner conflict in situations that may be unfair. Social jealousy can be managed by parents using the following rule: Never ignore your child's sentiments. Although you may not view drama over lunch sitting as a problem for your child, it can be a big deal to them. When your child begins to talk about the things that are bothering you, it's important to show empathy. Try explaining to your child, "I get how you might feel." Problem-solve your child's feelings by giving practical alternatives.

A second type of jealousy in young children is the belief that you will lose, or have lost, some love, attention, and security from another person due to someone or anything else. It could be their interest or commitment in an activity that takes too much of your time. This might manifest in the smallest settings such as when your youngster is clamoring to get the largest slice of birthday cake at a friend's celebration. If your child tears up when he doesn't get what they want (he's not the Birthday Boy after all), ask him why. Your child should be able to talk about his emotions and understand why they occur.

Dr. Zeltser said, "You want to affirm and recognize their feelings." "I'm sorry you were disappointed by the cake" and the "Sometimes we don’t get what we desire" statements are both acceptable. However, it's important to not begin the next sentence with the words "but", since this will make you reject their sentiments. Use "and" instead. It's okay to want the largest cake. Since it is your birthday today, we will let your buddy have it. Now, change the emphasis to something you think will make your kid happy. For example, encourage your son to tell your buddy how much he is having.

How to make life easier for your child: Parents should not tell their child to "Stop crying" or "Don't be unhappy". This isn't a way to help them. This is simply limiting their feelings and telling them to not display them. It's more important to teach them how to manage them.

This page was useful.

Chapter 14: How To Predict And Manage Your Children's Emotion

Enhance your child's ability to communicate with others emotionally

Emotions are strong and people will do or say things they wouldn't normally. This is what you do every day as a young child.

Emotional intelligence is about the ability to regulate one's feelings and emotions. The ability to regulate emotions is enhanced by experience. The majority of children begin to use methods to block out external stimuli around age 4. They close their eyes when they're afraid, and they stop hearing loud noises when they're scared.

It isn't until the age 10 when children start to adopt advanced techniques for emotional self regulation. These tactics can be broken down into two broad categories: those designed to fix the problem or those that attempt to tolerate the feeling.

Children can take action to fix a problem by becoming aware of it and creating a plan. When the situation seems overwhelming, they engage with emotion-focused coping. They try to endure and manage pain.

All these techniques are part of emotional Intelligence. Emotional Intelligence includes knowledge, awareness, and the ability of one to express and manage their emotions.

Although academic achievement in children has been the focus of most people's attention, emotional self regulation has been almost ignored. This is a horrible approach, given that evidence has shown emotional intelligence to be twice as effective as IQ in predicting eventual success.

A key aspect of emotional intelligence is self-control. This aspect is crucial in helping children to be successful. Children who are able regulate emotions and avoid distractions can be more productive and help others.

A remarkable study evaluated self-control in school-aged children and conducted follow-up examinations for those in their 30s. According to the research, self-control was more predictive of achievement than IQ and socioeconomic level. Also, self-control was associated with healthier children, higher earnings, and lower rates of alcoholism or criminal history.

Feelings serve a function

Awareness and comprehension of emotions are two aspects of emotional intelligence. To be able to regulate and express emotions we must first understand and accept our emotions. Emotions aren't an annoying part of human evolution, but serve a function.

According to the discrete theory on emotions, each major emotion was created to be independent and have a different purpose. This theory can then be used as a guideline for our conduct.

Sadness, a feeling that is particularly capable of slowing down our cognitive and bodily actions, is one example. This may give us an opportunity to think about the roots of our emotional turmoil.

Rage is the opposite. It speeds us up, generates energy, and sends blood to our extremities. This is an evolutionary step that sets us up to struggle, but in the current time it allows us to have continuous energy for fighting a different kind of battle. Anger alerts us when our rights are violated and helps us plan to defend ourselves against future threats.

We must acknowledge our feelings and meditate on them. Children's intense emotions at seemingly unimportant events are a good example of this. My child gets angry when she is unable to do something she was able previously, such as strapping her car seats independently.

In their recent policy statement, American Academy of Pediatrics urged parents not to use electronics as a method of controlling or subduing their child's emotions. They expressed concerns that the use of media as a method to relax might cause problems with boundary setting, or inability for youngsters to regulate their emotions.

To develop self-control, emotional intelligence, and emotional tolerance, children must be exposed to these emotions.

Enhancing your child's emotion intelligence

Researchers are now looking at ways caregivers can encourage emotional intelligence. In order to understand how emotional intelligence develops Dr. John Gottman studied how parents react when their children are upset. He discovered that parents respond to the emotions of their children in one of four ways.

Dismissing parents consider children's emotions to be insignificant and attempt to erase them quickly using distraction.

Parents who dislike bad feelings consider them to be something to crush, often by punishment.

Laissez-faire parent allow all emotions from child but fail help youngster to handle difficulties or establish boundaries.

Emotion coaching parents can be patient with children who express unpleasing emotions. Instead, they are able to use their emotional experience to connect by helping them name and solve the problem.

Dr. Gottman's studies show that children of parents who are emotional coaches are happier, more successful in school and have better relationships with their peers. The five basic methods that emotion coaches use to help their children cope with emotions are simple. Sometimes, this may take a very long time.

Dr. Gottman observed, however, that only 20-25% parents of emotion coaching clients followed all five phases. This suggests there is no need to guilt because no parent can accomplish this procedure in a single session.

Empathy coaching is as easy as practicing the five stages

Step 1 - Be aware of your child's emotions.

Parents who coach emotion are more aware of their children's emotions and can be sensitive to them. They don't expect their child will increase their emotional expression to make them feel better.

Click here to purchase this printable poster.

Step 2: Use emotions to teach and connect.

Emotions in children are neither a hassle nor a task. They are a way to get to know your child better and help them overcome difficult emotions.

Step 3 - Listen and validate your emotions

Your youngster deserves your full attention while you listen to what they are saying. Reflect on what you hear to ensure that your youngster can understand what you are hearing.

Step 4 - Label their feelings

After listening carefully, encourage your child to develop an awareness and vocabulary for emotional expression.

Step 5 - Help your youngster to think critically and set boundaries.

While all emotions are acceptable, not all acts are. Develop problem-solving capabilities to help your child deal with his/her emotions. Be specific about what you say. This requires that you help your youngster to identify their goals and find solutions.

Sometimes, emotions coaching is done quickly. These stages may take longer. Patience and patience are essential. If the issue involves a significant amount of work, you don't necessarily need to complete all five phases in one conversation.

Verywell Family

Emotional intelligence, also known as emotional intelligence (EQ), refers to a person's ability to control and express emotions well while being respectful of the feelings of others. It can be a set if abilities that children start to acquire at any time.

Emotional Intelligence: The Benefits

Research has proven that emotional intelligence offers many advantages that will help your child succeed throughout her entire life. These are just some of many benefits of emotional intelligence.

High IQ can be linked to high EQ. Children with higher emotional intelligence scores better on standardised examinations. They are more likely also to receive higher grades.

Improved connections. Children who have high emotional intelligence are better able to handle conflict and form closer connections. Adults who have high emotional intelligence report greater connections in their personal as well as professional lives.

The ability to feel good in childhood is associated with higher achievement throughout adulthood. An American Journal of Public Health study that covered 19 years showed that a child's kindergarten social and emotionally skills could predict long-term success. Children who are able to work together, share and follow instructions by the age of five are more likely to go to college and get a job after that age. 1

Greater mental health. A person with a higher level of emotional intelligence is less likely to develop depression or other mental diseases.

The benefits of emotional intelligence are obvious. An emotional intelligence-able youngster is more likely to do well in stressful situations. It is more likely that a child can communicate their feelings in a healthy manner than a child who yells at others or makes cruel comments when they're angry.

The good news is that all children are capable of developing emotional intelligence. They just need someone to teach them.

Label Your Child's Emotions

Knowing how your child feels is essential. You can help your child identify their emotions by giving them a name.

Your child might be sad that they had to part with a toy or a game. You can comment, "It appears like you're feeling pretty furious now." Is that correct?" If children seem upset, they can respond, "Are your feeling sorry that Grandma/Grandpa aren't coming to see you today?"

You can use emotional words like "angry", "upset," or "painful" to convey emotions. You should also include positive emotions such as "joy," excited," "thrilled," or "hopeful".

Building an emotional vocabulary

Show empathy

It's easy to overlook what your child is feeling when they're upset. However, disrespectful words can teach your child to be more aware of the negative feelings they're experiencing.

Better is to acknowledge their feelings and offer empathy. Even if you don't understand why they are unhappy, it's better. If your kid is crying because they were told they couldn't go the park until they cleaned their room, you can say something like "I get unhappy when it doesn't happen to me." It's sometimes hard to continue working when I don't feel like it.

If your child understands how you feel, they will be less inclined to display it through their actions. You can let your kid know that you understand their feelings and not make them cry.

How to Nurture empathysModel The Best Ways to Express Your Feelings

The ability to express one's feelings in a respectful manner is essential for kids. It's not okay to yell or throw objects, even if you say,

"My emotions have hurt", or draw a sad picture.

The best way to teach your child how to express emotions is to do it yourself.

Practice using emotional terms in your everyday communication and practicing talking about them. Speak something like "I get angry when I see children be mean on the playground" or "I get joy when we have our friends over for dinner."

Studies have shown that emotionally intelligent parents are much more likely to raise emotionally intelligent kids. Therefore, it is important to make it a priority to develop your talents in order for you to be a role model for your child.

Role Model the behavior that you want from your children

Teach Healthy Coping Skills

Understanding emotions is the first step to learning how to deal with them. Little ones might struggle to understand how to deal with stress, regain control, or face their fears.

Teach specialized skills. You might teach your child how to take deep breathes when they are angry to calm down their bodies. It's a kid-friendly method to teach them this. Have them take "bubble breathes" and inhale through the nose. Then, blow out through the mouth like they're blowing through bubble wands.

You can also help your youngster create a kit that helps manage their moods. There are many things that will help soothe their emotions and engage their senses. These include a coloring book or a favorite joke book. You can place the ornaments in a separate box. If they get upset, you can tell them to get their calm down kit so that they can practice using their tools for emotional regulation.

Teaching children how to deal with uncomfortable feelings

Develop problem-solving skills

Knowing how to resolve problems is a key part of emotional intelligence. Once you have acknowledged the sentiments and dealt with them, you can now work on how to resolve the issue.

Perhaps your youngster gets annoyed when their sibling interrupts them while they're playing video games. Discuss with them five solutions to this problem. The solutions do not have to be brilliant ideas. It is not necessary to have great ideas in the beginning.

Once they've identified at minimum five other options, encourage them each to consider the benefits and drawbacks. Then encourage them to select the best one.

Talk to your child about the mistakes they made and what you can do for them. Be a coach instead of a problem-solver. You can give instructions when needed but try to help your youngster realize that they can handle difficult situations on their own.

Teaching children how they can solve their own problems

Make emotional intelligence an ongoing goal

No matter how bright your child's emotional intelligence, there is always the possibility for them to grow. There are bound to be some challenges during childhood and young adulthood. As they grow older, children will be faced with challenges that may test their skills. It's a good idea to make skill-building a priority in your daily life. Talk to your child about emotions everyday, even when he is young.

Talk about the emotions characters might experience in novels and movies. Discuss how to better address issues or what tactics characters might use for respect.

As your kid ages, you can start talking about real-world issues with them. Make it a regular conversation.

You can use your child's mistakes to help you grow. Talk with your child about ways they can improve their behavior. Your support and guidance can help your child develop the emotional intelligence, mental strength and perseverance they need to be successful in their lives.

Chapter 15: Tips On Managing Your Child's Emotions And Feelings

The ability to manage major emotions is largely a function of age and growth. Sometimes it is just part of who you are to feel things more strongly.

Young children can have a difficult time managing their emotions. You can teach your child how to manage emotions and build emotional awareness.

Teach your child all about emotions

It is crucial that your youngster understands and describes how they feel.

1. Teach children about emotions.

Say, "You seem unwell right now," and "I can see you are mad." Or, express your feelings with "I'm sorry we can't go to Grandma's today" and "I'm shocked those guys were being that cruel today."

Discussions about characters on TV and in novels may spark conversations about sentiments. Ask your child questions, such as "How do this character feel?" As you practice, your child will be able to name their emotions better.

The ability to feel emotions clearly can help kids be emotionally strong.

Building an emotional vocabulary

Separate Feelings Vs. Behaviors

It is important that children learn to express their emotions in a socially acceptable manner. For example, screaming in the middle the grocery store, complaining or throwing a tantrum at school are not acceptable.

Let children know that they can feel any emotion they like, and that it's okay to be very angry or terrified. Children have many options for how they respond to these unpleasant sensations.

However, they do not have the right of being angry at someone. It's possible for toddlers to be disappointed if their favorite ice cream isn't available at the shop, but it's not okay to run around screaming and bothering other children.

Discipline behaviour, but not emotions. For example, you might say "You are going time-out because your brother struck you." Or "You are losing the toy for the rest day because you are screaming and it hurts our ears."

Be firm with your child about their behavior and not their emotions

Validate and Link

Sometimes parents can underestimate their child's emotions. It's okay to say "Stop being so angry!" It's nothing major.

This will tell your youngster that they are not being inappropriate. They are fine, even if you think they are out of proportion.

Indicate whether you feel they are sad, angry, embarrassed, ashamed, disappointed, or sad. Then, you can show empathy and understand their feelings.

Even though you may be saying, "I am sorry, we aren’t going to park today," it may come off as too harsh.

Instead, you can say, "I'm sorry we're not going to the parks today. Your youngster will be reassured that they may experience some feelings from time to time even though they might not be as intense or frequent.

Encourage your child to understand that emotions are temporary. They won't be there forever, or for very long.

It might be helpful for young children to recognize that emotions as well as tears can come and gone.

Acceptance

It's not uncommon to have difficulty understanding how to handle highly emotional young people. It's common to feel confused or overwhelmed by it all.

While you may not always understand why your child feels certain emotions, it's a good idea to let them know that you are aware of their feelings and that that is OK.

Children must learn to perceive, understand and deal effectively with what they are feeling.

Some people may consider extremely sensitive young children "wimps" and assume that they can be cured. This is not only dangerous but also inaccurate. Crying and feeling angry are not bad things. They are not signs of weakness.

Everyone is different and each person's temperament is unique.

2 Help your child to understand that you accept them for what they are.

Teach Emotion Regulation

Emotion control is dependent on the development of your child. Children's ability to regulate behavior is often limited before they reach 24 months old. 3

But this does not mean you cannot teach children how emotions should be handled. Many children can begin to manage their emotions as soon as they start preschool. 3

Here are some tips to teach your child how to manage their emotions.

Deep breathing is important. Teaching your child to deep breathe is a good idea. Try telling them to "smell a rose, then blow up the balloon". This can be done with them only a few times during distress. Encourage them to use it independently as needed.

To calm down, count. Encourage your child to use counting to distract her from negative thoughts. These mental pursuits can be used to reduce anxiety.

You should take a break. You can give your child some time out or ask the teacher if they would like to go outside of class for water or solitude if they feel they need it. Be clear with your child that they can do this, before they get sent to jail for their misbehavior. Then they can decide when it's time to leave.

A calm-down kit can be created. Make a calm-down box. Fill it with items that can help your child calm down (or brighten things up) (or cheer you up). A few of the things that might help calm your child are coloring books and crayons as well as scratch-and sniff stickers and photos that they love.

You can work together to solve the problem with your child. You can work with your child to address any issues they may have. Ask them to give you their opinions on possible solutions. They might come up with innovative solutions together.

Identify mood enhancers. Talk to your child about activities that make them feel happy. Note these activities and share them with your kid. If they feel down, you can encourage them to try one of these exercises to help with their emotions.

7 Ways to Help Your Child Cope with Anger

Avoid reinforcing outbursts

Your response to your child's emotions is a powerful influence. Sometimes parents allow their children to be emotional and have outbursts. If your goal is to help your child manage their emotions better, this is a good thing to avoid.

Rewarding your youngster for calming down:

Give your child a gift for every effort she makes. They may find that shouting at their sibling or breaking down in tears is an effective way to get something they desire.

Your youngster deserves your attention. It's not a good idea to teach your youngster that anger is the best method of attracting your attention.

Calm your toddler every now and again:

It's important to provide comfort. However, it's equally important that your child learns the skills to calm down and manage their emotions.

Remind your child to stop crying

You could make your child more miserable if you tell him to stop crying. You might make your kids feel worse if you get too upset by their tears.

Admit that your youngster is sensitive

It's possible to send a message to parents by telling every coach, teacher, friend that your child is sensitive. It is a good idea to have some insight into the temperament of your child, but it is not mandatory. You should only share this information with your child if you think it will help them adjust their approach or provide some insight. It's important to keep the conversation positive, such as "My child experiences incredible emotions."

Challenging Your Child

While you may believe it's possible to avoid distressing experiences for your child, there will be times. If you find out that a disturbing movie is being shown at your sleepover, you can encourage your child to quit if they aren't able to recover from it.

But, it is not productive to exempt your child from every difficult struggle and all the realities of living. Your kid must have the ability to deal with a wide range of emotions in a variety contexts for their success and happiness.

You may be thinking of letting your child skip school field day because they have difficulty controlling their anger and fear that they will experience a breakdown if their kickball team loses. Although it may sound appealing, it is likely that such a situation will occur more than once in your life. Experience managing it might be extremely helpful.

Don't try to shield them from every challenge. Give them enough space to express themselves. Listen to your gut instincts about what is best for your kid.

When you should seek professional assistance

Research shows that although emotional regulation begins in infancy, most children need to master it by age 8.

4 Therefore, even children who aren’t naturally emotional may experience a time when the tears just keep coming down or their temper flares up.

It is possible that there is no cause for alarm. However it is still worth visiting your doctor to ensure there aren't any medical conditions, psychological issues, or undiagnosed ear infections. This is particularly important for children who are small or have trouble communicating.

You don't need to fear if your child is always emotional. If your child suddenly has more difficulty controlling their emotions, talk to your doctor.

If your child has trouble managing their emotions, you can seek professional assistance.

5 If they start to sob so often that it is difficult for them to focus in class, or if they struggle to maintain friendships due their anger management skills, they might be looking for additional help.

Studies have shown a link between dysregulation and a variety mental health disorders as children get older. This includes anything from sadness, anxiety, drug addiction, suicide thought, attention deficit hyperactivity (ADHD), or violence.

6

Experts believe that therapies that target self-regulation may aid children's development.

Once the problem has been diagnosed, you might take actions to teach your child how to manage emotions at crucial moments. Talk to your child's team about the best methods for you to achieve that goal.

A word from Verywell

Keep in mind that emotional control is something that young children still need to learn. Although it is an inherent tendency for some kids to feel too emotional, others may not realize this.

You might be all your child needs to learn to manage their emotions in a responsible way. While the process can seem intimidating at times it is worth it for your child's benefit over time.

You should also remember that this could be a good thing. Children who are extremely emotional often experience intense emotions. While your emotionally ill child may experience extreme anger and vengeance, they might also be extremely compassionate and passionate leaders. A level 10 person may feel aggravation, but may also feel joy and excitement.

Children, just like adults, have emotions. While we try to raise well-rounded children, it's vital that they are able to regulate their emotions.

This is essential as children who have trouble regulating their emotions may become conflictive with their peers, their families, and, eventually, be excluded from their group activities.

Recognizing feelings is crucial in helping your child regulate his emotions. It will be difficult to help your child control his emotions if they are not aware of the sensations they are experiencing.

It might be helpful to start teaching your child the difference between happy, sad and furious. Once you have everything sorted out, your child can learn relaxation strategies to manage negative emotions like anger and fear. You could use counting to ten or taking deep, slow breaths.

Speaking to your child when they have unpleasant emotions is crucial. This will help them understand and find ways to overcome it. Although verbal signals are useful, parents must recognize when it's important to use nonverbal cues in order to communicate a message.

Children who experience anger, sadness, stress or anger can respond differently.

Some children may prefer to stay home while others may choose not to. Others may bite their lips, pick at their hair, throw objects around or pick their noses. As they learn to manage their emotions, it is essential to understand when verbal and non-verbal cues come into play.

Although there may be some environmental factors contributing to your child's emotional response, you can find a way to change them. Perhaps your child isn't getting enough sleep. This can cause them to become cranky and angry. Limit screen time in the evening and use other techniques that help children fall asleep easier to fix this problem.

Your child's exercise routine can be a preventative measure. You may also find it helpful to eat healthy meals and snack regularly. It may help to talk with your child about how you can make the situation more manageable. The use of noise-canceling headphones might help if you have anxiety when it is loud or in crowded situations.

You might consider creating a card or chart that your child can use to remind you of the tactics. One example is a printed letter you might give your child that says, "When I feel sad or upset, I need three deep breaths and squeeze my stress ball."

Cartoon imagery depicting happiness can be used to calm and soothe your child if they are unable to read.

This can help you build stronger relationships with your child and enable them to participate in more social activities. Also, let them know how happy it is to see them respond with maturity to difficult situations and manage their emotions.

There are ways parents can change the emotions of their kids positively

When raising children to be well-rounded people, parents need emotional intelligence. It is a combination of the child's personality, family dynamics, parenting style, as well as other aspects.

What is Emotional Intelligence?

Researchers have been discussing the concept of emotion intelligence since the 1980s. According to the argument, general intelligence (IQ) refers to your ability and ability to process information to make good decisions. Emotional intelligence (EQ), on the other hand, refers to your ability and ability to deal with emotions.

It is the ability of understanding, using and managing emotions in positive ways. It's a higher level of emotional intelligence that can assist intentional parents in being more purposeful in their parenting.

Research suggests that a higher level of emotional intelligence leads to greater health, academic achievement, stronger relationships, and better overall health. It is a learned, scientifically-based skill set that benefits children.

Emotional Intelligence, Self-Awareness

Emotional intelligence is about having self-awareness. This is crucial for parents who want to be intentional and productive parents.

Self-awareness refers to understanding yourself and your behavior in relation to what you are doing, how it feels and what it isn't.

This is a great starting place as an individual and as a foundation upon which you can build on other skills. Being an intentional parent means being self-aware, understanding your motivations, and being able to identify your goals.

Emotional Intelligence & Parenting

As it relates the world of emotions, there are two kinds of parents: Emotion Dismissing and Parenting. Emotion dismissing parents are action-oriented. They don't want emotions. They view emotions as being destructive for their children and them. The opposite is true for emotion-coaching parent: they are open to emotions and can explore them with others.

Research showed that children with different kinds of parents had very different life paths. Two children with the same IQ would achieve completely different educational achievements at age 8, if their parents had high emotional intelligence.

How to Parent With Emotional Intelligence

1. Make a schedule with your children

Children thrive when routine is established and they know what to do. Schedules were often forgotten, especially during the latest lockdown. But, an anxiety or stress-level increase can result from a lack of knowledge. Many of my clients, parents and friends eventually see the value of schedules for peace and balance. Schedules can be used as a guide to help people know what to expect. They also reduce anxiety and confusion.

2. Limit your exposure to negativity and screen time

Many parents keep the news channel on all hours, which exposes their home to negative news and images nearly every hour. There are more negative news stories available than ever. It is important to keep up to date with what is happening. However, you don't need to be consuming it constantly. This is a constant influence on everyone's moods.

3. Create your family's digital well-being plan

Screen time 24 hours a week is not healthy. Make sure you have screen-free hours and that there are limits. You can teach your children to be responsible digital citizens. This includes eating the right digital diet. It is a fact that too much screen time can negatively affect your mental health and mood. If you have not done so already, make a family's digital well-being plan. Let this guide screen use in your house. Being a parent with emotional intelligence means that you're aware of the consequences of screen time for you and your kids.

4. Mental health is a priority

The Emotional Intelligence Hack for Parents is to Prioritize Mental Health for the Family.

Particularly considering what has happened during pandemic. Everywhere you look, there's an update on the COVID case count; new variants or lockdown measures. I recommend parents that their children keep their eyes on the things they can control. This includes their mind, attitude, and actions.

Effective parenting involves communication and relationship.

5. It is important to not ignore their worries or anxiety

Be active in listening with empathy. Take the time to understand your child's emotions. So they can be guided in the right direction, or you can teach them better coping techniques. Teach your children to recognize that no emotion is good or worse. Instead, it is what your children do with your emotion that matters.

Parents can support their children by leading conversations. Instead of asking one-sided questions, like "How are your days?" you can ask your child, "What was the most memorable thing that happened at school today?" This leads to more discussion.

We are all faced with complex emotions as parents. While some parents are able to ignore their emotions, others can give their children too much power. Instead, look at emotions as information. "Oh, that's interesting. I wonder what this feeling really means." This attitude of curiosity helps us discover value and insight in our feelings while we step back from reacting.

6. Quality time

Spend quality time together as a family every single day! You can't afford being too busy and trying to do everything at once. It will only affect your family bonding. Spend time together praying, talking, sharing, playing boardgames, and eating meals. As a family, make it a priority that you spend quality time doing what is most enjoyable. In order to foster family bonding, you should also establish traditions and rituals.

7. Encourage physical movement

Exercise releases feel-goodhormones. Endorphins are another hormone that can trigger positive emotions in the body. Family fitness should involve everyone in the family and everyone should get active. If you or your children are still at work, it is crucial for them to move and get some exercise.

8. Assemble goals

We humans want to accomplish many things in our lives. But, many people don't know how to set SMART goals. These are goals that can help you get what you want. Intentional parents teach their children the art to set goals. This activates the road towards emotional intelligence. Your family can be your most reliable accountability partner. This is especially true for those who have shared goals they want to achieve together.

9. Sleep

It cannot be stressed enough how important quality sleep is. Everyone should get enough quality sleep. There is a guideline that you can use to determine how much sleep, depending on your age. You can get your kids to agree on a bedtime schedule. What time should they be asleep? Digital well-being is dependent on your ability to shut down screens an hour before you go to bed. A lack of sleep can have a negative impact on emotions and behaviour.

10. Nutrition

The quality of the food you eat has an impact on your mental, physical, and spiritual state. A healthy, balanced diet is essential to ensure that your body gets the proper nutrients it needs to thrive. Emotional Intelligence is about a healthy understanding of your emotions. This can't be separated from nutrition. Did you realize that many digestive issues have an emotional origin?

Finally, research shows that sharing meals can protect us from depression. A lot of evidence supports the notion that depression can be caused by a lack of social connection. A major trigger for depression is feeling lonely, isolated, and not included in the community. So make mealtimes an intimate family affair and eat mindfully.

Children raised by emotionally intelligent parents are more capable of navigating stressful and complex situations. They have positive and healthy relationships, which is a plus. Children who have been raised by emotionally accessible parents are more resilient than their peers and can feel calm inside. They also tend to have a better outlook for the future, and they are more likely to make a difference in their community.

Emotional intelligence is a skill that can be acquired over time. Parents are the best people to teach these world-changing, life-changing skills.

This article will discuss the effects of parental reactions on children's behavior.

Being a parent to a young baby is an emotionally charged experience. There's the pure joy in cuddling, playing, laughing, exploring, learning, and enjoying your baby's new discoveries. There are also the struggles--the stress, anger frustration and resentment at not understanding a baby's cry and how to calm it down, at the completely irrational demands of toddlers or the aggressive behavior displayed by older children toward a new child. These experiences are bound to elicit strong feelings, which can be difficult for parents to handle.

These feelings are important and it is crucial that you pay attention. It is the way you react to these situations that will determine your child's future development. Your response will affect his ability learn and manage coping skills. It will also influence his future behavior. Imagine a 2-yearold child who is unable to cope with the fact his breakfast cereal was served in a blue container instead of his red. This is a normal part of toddler life. Reacting with anger or frustration can only make the situation worse and not help the child to calm down and cope. One of the best ways to reduce your distress, and that of your child, is to learn how you react. It also helps children manage their emotions. This will make them more successful in school, and help them build friendships.

It can be difficult to manage strong, negative emotions. It is worth the effort for your child and you. These are some tips and guidelines to help you understand the best strategies.

Tune into your feelings.

There is no right or wrong way to feel. What you do with your emotions can make a difference in how they are used. What is most important is to recognize your feelings and make a decision about how you want to respond.

Take behavior into account in relation to your child's temperament and development.

Because the meaning that you assign to your child's behavior has an impact on how you handle your emotions and reactions to that behavior, it is essential to set appropriate expectations. If you consider the behavior manipulative or hurtful (i.e., biting and hitting), then your reaction will likely be to escalate rather than to calm your child. Extremely angry responses rarely teach children coping skills. When you view these behaviors in the context normal development, it is easier to approach your child and show empathy. You will be more likely to respond calmly.

Remember: You cannot force your child to do something-- eat or sleep, poop, talk, stop throwing tantrums.

However, you have no control over their actions. It is up to you to respond to them. This will determine and guide their behavior. If throwing tantrums results in more TV time, a later sleeptime, or simply more of your attention (a primary goal if older siblings are dealing with major rivalry), then your toddler is putting 2 + 2 together and making an important assessment: "Tantrums actually work!" Excellent strategy! You can put that one in your win column."

It all together

The Scenario

Jonah, three-year-old, says to Lauren, "You are a mean mommy, and you hate me." Lauren then kicks Jonah after Lauren tells him that playdate is over. Liam must go home.

Step 1 - Listen to your feelings

Lauren is angry and wants to shout: "You are most ungrateful child ever! Liam has been here 2 hours. I have set aside everything I needed for you to watch, make cookies, set up your painting project, and so on. It's never enough!" However, she is aware that her anger will not help her child and only increase their suffering. She takes deep breaths and contemplates how to respond in order to help Jonah to control his emotions and accept what is happening.

Step 2--Validate your child and tune in to them:

This is where setting appropriate expectations comes into play. Lauren reminds Jonah that even at age 3, children are still heavily driven by their emotions. She explains that her goal is for Jonah to learn how to handle life's disappointments. She tells him calmly that she knows he is upset about Liam having to go home. You and he have so much fun together. It's always difficult when playdates end. But you will still be okay" It is vital to communicate your confidence that your child can manage his difficult feelings. By trying to make everything better, you can inadvertently convey that your child cannot handle disappointment. It makes it less likely that this skill will be learned.

Step 3: Don't let your child throw out bait.

Young children will employ any strategy they can to get what their parents want. For example, they might use extra TV or dessert to get more. You can ignore behaviors that aren't serving your child in real life. This means Lauren won't respond to Jonah’s request, "You are meanest mommy ." She doesn't allow it distract attention from the limit she has set, which is usually to control other people's actions and avoid things that the child is uncomfortable.

Step 4: Define the limit and make choices

It's okay to be angry and sad, but it's wrong to kick. Kicking hurts. I understand that you don't wish to hurt me. Your body is just trying to control your emotions. You can either take a break so you can calm yourself down or help with the dinner preparations. Lauren will let Jonah know that she can handle his feelings of sadness and frustration and that she believes he can manage to calm himself. Jonah is left with two choices: stay angry or gather his thoughts and spend time with his mom.

Manage your emotions effectively and calmly.

RESILIENT KIDS WILL BE BUILT IF YOU ARE AWARE OF YOUR CHILD'S FEELINGS

The most important task of parenthood is teaching children how to handle their emotions. All children go through times of stress in life. Children need to have the ability to handle it. Children's emotional resilience or the ability to cope with their emotions, is vital to their long-term happiness and well-being. Emotional Resilience includes six key skills. These include being able or able acknowledge and accept feelings, how to express them appropriately, developing positive outlooks, being capable of dealing with negative emotions and managing stressful life events.

RECOGNIZING and ACCEPTING FEELINGS

Attitudes & emotions

As a child develops, they learn from the world around and receive messages and information that will influence how they understand and express their feelings.

Below are some simple tips to help children improve their development.

Accept different emotions – Children often receive the unwritten message, that happy is the only acceptable emotion. Try your best to acknowledge and embrace other emotions.

Accept all emotions. Allowing children to know it is okay for them to feel difficult emotions such as sadness, madness, disappointment, and frustration.

Talk about emotions - Talk about them frequently. It is easy to get these conversations started by pointing at the characters they love on their favorite shows or books.

Let your emotions be known - It is OK to show emotion from time to another.

Encourage your child to recognize emotions. You can tell your child what you are seeing, hearing or feeling that makes you believe they feel a specific emotion.

EXPRESSFEELINGS APPROPRIATELY

Children learn from watching and this holds true for learning how to manage, express, and cope with emotions. Children watch us adults as we react to both small and large emotions. It is important to try our best, and model appropriate ways to express and manage emotion. Acceptable methods of expressing emotions should be consistent with cultural and family norms. Children need to be exposed to rituals and traditions that are related to emotions. How their culture and families deal with celebration and loss is taught through funerals, festivals and weddings.

Talk with your child about emotions. Talk to your child about your feelings when they begin to talk to it. Give them all of your attention and stop what you're doing.

With the classic sentence starter "It feels like you feel ..."."", you can sum up what they have shared with you.

Be kind and reward children who express their emotions in a mature way. I think you handled your anger well. "I saw you get very upset. Take deep breaths and walk away. Wow!"

Handle inappropriate expressions - Determine how you will deal with the hurtful, disrespectful, yelling or swearing behavior of others. Best for children is to set clear consequences that allow them to learn acceptable ways of expressing themselves.

Recognize and acknowledge the negative emotion.

Tell them precisely and clearly what you want them to stop doing. It should be brief, concise, and straight to the point.

Implement a logical consequence like quiet time to encourage self-regulation.

positive_thinking_how_to_foster

BUILDING A POSITIVE OPERATION

What children think about and believe is directly related to how they feel. They can only draw on the lessons they have learned. Through optimism, parents can help their children build a positive self-image.

Encourage optimism. This skill can be taught and encouraged. We need to be an example of optimism. Encourage children to set realistic goals, and encourage them to use creativity and initiative in reaching those goals. This skill is taught when children are able to find and participate in activities that they like.

Encourage curiosity. - Curiosity can be a real challenge for parents. They may ask "why", take things apart, or get into things they wish they wouldn't. Remember the previous statement? Keep your optimism and view curiosity as a strength. It is through curiosity that children discover and become interested about the world around us. You can encourage this by supporting their interest in new activities and letting them discover the world around you. Ask questions when they're excited about something and be available to show it.

Encourage contentment. Teaching children how to accept, tolerate and appreciate what they have can help them be content. Demonstrate gratitude and appreciation. Talk to your children about the highlights from their day. Encourage empathy, and discuss other people's viewpoints. Discussion of accepting what is beyond our control and how we can change it. Boredom is acceptable.

DEVELOPING COPING SKILLS

Coping skills are the tools that we use to control our emotions, and solve problems that may be causing negative emotions.

Help Your Child to Be a Problem Solver. Parents can fall into the trapof trying to solve all of their children's problems. We do not want our children to be upset. Sometimes, it is better to do things ourselves. Children are encouraged to experience the "yuck" part of life. Ask them questions that will help develop their ability to solve problems themselves. Encourage them to solve their problem. This lets them know that you believe they can solve it.

You can help your child learn relaxation. So many of our days revolve around go, do, do, go. Learning the skill of relaxation is a must. Set a good example of how stress can be managed by taking care yourself and taking some time to relax. Many apps and websites can be used to help with yoga, belly breathing, relaxation, and other activities.

Help your child Look for Support. - Talk with children about the fact that everyone should talk about their feelings, particularly if they become overwhelming. It's important to find safe people to talk with. They should be able to talk to a trusted friend, family member or teacher.

www.ingramcontent.com/pod-product-compliance
Lightning Source LLC
Chambersburg PA
CBHW071338120626
46546CB00002B/608

* 9 7 8 1 9 9 8 7 6 9 3 5 3 *